# How to Co-Teach

# How to Co-Teach

## A Guide for General and Special Educators

by

**Elizabeth A. Potts, Ph.D.**
University of Virginia
Northern Virginia Center
Falls Church

and

**Lori A. Howard, Ph.D.**
University of Virginia
Northern Virginia Center
Falls Church

·P A U L·H·
BROOKES
PUBLISHING Co ®

Baltimore • London • Sydney

Paul H. Brookes Publishing Co.
Post Office Box 10624
Baltimore, Maryland 21285-0624
USA

www.brookespublishing.com

Typeset by Integrated Publishing Solutions, Grand Rapids, Michigan.
Manufactured in the United States of America by
Sheridan Books, Inc., Chelsea, Michigan.

Cover image © Masterfile.

The individuals and situations described in this book and the accompanying DVD are based on real
people. Some names and identifying details have been changed to protect confidentiality. Real names
are used with permission.

**Library of Congress Cataloging-in-Publication Data**

Potts, Elizabeth A.
   How to co-teach : a guide for general and special educators / by Elizabeth A. Potts and
   Lori A. Howard.
      p.      cm.
   Includes bibliographical references and index.
   ISBN-13: 978-1-59857-169-1 (pbk.)
   ISBN-10: 1-59857-169-9 (pbk.)
   1. Teaching teams.   I. Howard, Lori A.   II. Title.
   LB1029.T4P68 2011
   371.14'8—dc22                                                        2011012177

British Library Cataloguing in Publication data are available from the British Library.

2015   2014   2013   2012   2011

10    9    8    7    6    5    4    3    2    1

# Contents

# About the Forms on the Accompanying DVD

In addition to video clips, the accompanying DVD contains printable versions of eight forms from *How to Co-Teach* that are intended to facilitate collaborative planning and instruction.

Purchasers of *How to Co-Teach* may print the forms from a computer for their own use. Purchasers may also choose to make photocopies of the forms printed from an original DVD. Refer to the End User License Agreement for details.

To access the forms, double-click the DVD icon on your computer's desktop. Once the screen opens, double-click the folder named "Printable Forms." Then, double-click "Start.pdf."

All of the forms on this DVD are provided in PDF format and may be printed easily by clicking on the appropriate bookmark, selecting "Print," and typing the corresponding page number(s). Purchasers may also save these forms to a computer to print as needed, in accordance with the terms of the End User License Agreement that they accepted when they accessed this feature of the DVD.

The following printable forms are found on the accompanying DVD:

- A Co-Teacher's Oath
- Co-Teaching Planning Checklist
- Lesson Plan Organizer
- Seating Chart Progress Monitoring Form
- Exit Slip Tracking Form
- Curriculum-Based Measurement Tracking Form
- Co-Teaching Self-Assessment
- K-W-L Chart

# About the Authors

**Elizabeth A. Potts, Ph.D.,** earned a bachelor of science degree in liberal studies and a master's degree in education, with an emphasis on special education, from Longwood College in Virginia. She earned a doctoral degree with an emphasis on mild disabilities from the University of Virginia. Dr. Potts is an assistant professor and a program director for special education programs at the University of Virginia Northern Virginia Center.

**Lori A. Howard, Ph.D.,** earned a master's degree in educational audiology from the University of Northern Colorado. She began her career in special education working with students who are deaf and have hearing impairments. Subsequently, she earned a doctoral degree from the University of Virginia in educational psychology. Dr. Howard teaches special education courses related to collaboration and instruction, teaming, consultation, and individualized education program development in the special education program at the University of Virginia Northern Virginia Center. She has also taught special education curriculum and methods courses at George Mason University in Fairfax, Virginia.

# Acknowledgments

We would like to thank the teachers who graciously allowed us to videotape them talking about their co-teaching experiences. We appreciate their candor and willingness to share their practices.

We also extend most sincere and considerable gratitude to Ben Eckman, the DVD guru. Truly, without your expertise and great assistance the crazy idea that was the DVD would not have come to fruition. Thank you, also, to Ben's family for allowing us to steal some of his precious "free" time with you.

We would also like to thank Rebecca Lazo for her guidance and vision that helped to bring this book to fruition. In addition, we extend our thanks to Stephen Plocher, who provided careful editing/proofing that helped to ensure that our words were in our voice.

We have had invaluable assistance in understanding the daily rigors and joys of co-teaching by every co-teacher who shared his or her story with us. These stories provided our inspiration.

Finally, we must acknowledge the support of our families. Our spouses were unflagging in their support, even providing take-out dinner when necessary. When Lori needed a break, there was a furry golden retriever who insisted on a refreshing game of fetch.

# Foreword

The era of the No Child Left Behind Act of 2001 (NCLB; PL 107-110) and the emphasis on accountability at all levels that came with it have left many clear marks on educational practice. Among the most tangible changes in practice observed in the first decade of the 21st century is the increasing inclusion of students with disabilities in general education classrooms. To be sure, a move toward inclusive education had been afoot since at least the 1990s, if not before. But the NCLB era brought specific emphasis to providing students with disabilities access to the general curriculum and having instruction delivered by highly qualified teachers. This renewed focus on accountability, higher standards, and meaningful access to higher level content—not just physical access to general education classrooms—was felt especially at the middle and high school levels, where focus on content was already a point of increasing effort, emphasis, and scrutiny. It is not surprising that co-teaching is becoming one of the most prevalent ways to provide students with disabilities access to the general education curriculum through highly qualified teachers. Co-teaching, in theory, involves the collaboration of two highly qualified teachers (one highly qualified in teaching the content and the other highly qualified in making the curriculum accessible). However, based on several qualitative studies, we know that co-teaching is rarely implemented the way it was intended (Scruggs, Mastropieri, & McDuffie, 2007), primarily due to lack of training that is necessary to be able to effectively co-teach. Such training should be multifaceted and ongoing, and this book provides the foundation for such training.

In addition to providing a firm foundation in the rationale and conceptual underpinnings of co-teaching as an instructional delivery model, the book provides practical strategies that help teachers not only grasp the conceptual foundations but also take those concepts and apply them in their classroom. It is noteworthy that the book covers all aspects of effective co-teaching, including such matters as how to effectively communicate and plan, as well as how to effectively teach in a co-taught setting. Communication and planning ahead of time are critical elements of successful co-teaching, though these may be easy to underestimate or even overlook as schools and teams move toward implementing co-teaching. Perhaps more important, this text offers what others often miss when debating the merits of co-teaching: effective instruction. Although research on co-teaching is still in an emergent phase, it seems safe to conclude that whatever the teaching arrangement, or whatever co-teaching model is chosen, there are elements of effective instruction that we know are associated with improved student outcomes. Where this text is unique is in the authors' attention to not only the critical elements of co-teaching but also to 1) a description of what effective instruction should look like in a co-taught classroom and 2) explicit strategies for implementing this effective instruction in a co-taught setting. Furthermore, Potts and Howard directly address another issue others may gloss over: the discrepancy between the ideal way to implement co-teaching versus the realistic way co-teaching is likely to be implemented in schools today.

They provide practical strategies to ensure that co-teaching is implemented as effectively as possible given the vagaries of school variables that may be beyond the control of the individual teacher (e.g., situations in which one teacher co-teaches with multiple teachers during the same instructional time).

The book is organized around five main themes, which include 1) respect for the perspectives of others, 2) the need to practice communication, 3) an explicit focus on classroom teaching, 4) an emphasis on building student success, and 5) ongoing efforts to improve and reflect on relationships. In the first section, the authors provide a brief description of co-teaching and common co-teaching models. In addition, they thoroughly describe one of the underlying premises of co-teaching: taking advantage of the unique strengths that general education and special education teachers bring to the co-teaching relationship. Often in co-teaching, teachers do not appreciate the different perspectives of general versus special education teachers, but these differences have been shown to be vital to the successful co-teaching relationship.

Typically, the general education teacher has expertise in the content as well as the scope and sequencing of instruction. The special education teacher has expertise on how to teach based on students' unique learning needs and how to adapt instruction so all students can learn. The special education teacher should also be familiar with a number of instructional strategies that could be effective for all students. Unfortunately, we also know that these effective or adapted instructional strategies are rarely implemented in co-taught settings (Scruggs et al., 2007). Potts and Howard address this with thorough explanations of the different strengths each teacher brings and how to utilize those strengths in a co-teaching arrangement. Furthermore, they provide descriptions of effective practices that could be easily implemented in a co-taught classroom. The last chapter in this section pertains to the importance of volunteering for co-teaching, which is yet another aspect of the process that may be diminished or overlooked. It should go without saying that teachers who volunteer are more likely to be in a place where they are open to new ideas, sharing teaching responsibilities, and trying new approaches than would be teachers who are told that they are going to co-teach. Administrators in particular would be wise to heed the advice offered in this section.

In the second section, Potts and Howard focus on communication, the key to effective co-teaching. Instead of just stating that effective communication needs to occur between co-teachers, they thoroughly describe the components of effective communication and provide practical strategies to ensure that effective communication is occurring. They even discuss how to have difficult conversations with a co-teaching partner. Furthermore, they provide a list of questions that should be answered and discussed prior to co-teaching in order to build a stable, productive co-teaching relationship. They conclude with an extraordinarily useful co-planning checklist and lesson planning organizer, which would be invaluable to both beginning and veteran co-teachers.

In the third section, Potts and Howard focus on classroom teaching. Again, the beauty of their coverage here lies in their emphasis on some foundational aspects of effective instruction; they just happen to provide this in the context of co-teaching. In this section, they discuss the importance of assessment and ensuring that both formative and summative assessments are used to guide and evaluate the effects of instruction. In addition, they discuss the need for co-teachers to thoroughly review all aspects of grading and student evaluation and how they might differentiate grading within their co-taught class. The authors provide sample adapted rubrics for students with disabilities. A particularly useful guide is offered in the form of an outline of several common grading issues that teachers frequently confront, along with a list of pros and cons for each issue.

In the fourth section, Potts and Howard discuss the importance of all teachers focusing on building student success. Again, regardless of how compatible co-teachers may be, implementing effective instruction is the key to a successful co-taught classroom, and this emphasis is what makes this book unique. In this section in particular, the authors go to great lengths to describe the components of effective instruction and provide explicit descriptions of research-based instructional strategies for inclusive elementary, middle, and high school classrooms. To the authors' credit, they rightly provide equal focus on establishing a positive classroom climate through effective classroom management and behavior management techniques.

In the fifth and final section, Potts and Howard discuss the importance of reflection on co-teaching. A clear emphasis throughout their text is the need for co-teachers to commit not only to a new or different approach to teaching but also to a process that is ongoing and reflective. Toward that end, these authors suggest that co-teachers keep a reflection journal. Each chapter has questions for co-teachers to reflect on, and these are differentiated based on the teachers' experience with co-teaching. Beyond simple reflection, Potts and Howard suggest that co-teachers should set goals and monitor their growth on a regular basis. They are further advised to complete self-assessments pertaining to co-teaching and to discuss ways to improve their co-teaching relationship on an ongoing basis. These are critical components of maintaining an effective co-teaching relationship.

In conclusion, the uniqueness of *How to Co-Teach* makes it a must for all co-teachers. It provides a thorough overview of all co-teaching topics associated with co-teaching success. Beyond the larger conceptual issues, it provides practical suggestions for classroom use, and it provides explicit strategies that teachers can easily use in their own co-taught classrooms (including the accompanying DVD of video clip examples and handouts; these provide excellent tools for both teachers and trainers). But perhaps most appreciated is the recurring emphasis on research-based instructional and management strategies, which, after all, are far more important to student success than the particular instructional arrangement teachers choose to use.

*Kimberly McDuffie-Landrum, Ph.D.*
*Assistant Professor, School of Education*
*Bellarmine University, Louisville, Kentucky*

## REFERENCES

No Child Left Behind Act of 2001, PL 107-110, 115 Stat. 1425, 20 U.S.C. §§ 6301 *et seq.*
Scruggs, T.E., Mastropieri, M.A., & McDuffie, K.A. (2007). Co-teaching in inclusive classrooms: A meta-synthesis of qualitative research. *Exceptional Children, 73,* 392–416.

# Introduction

*Coming together is a beginning. Keeping together is progress.*
*Working together is success.* (Henry Ford)

Since the late 1990s, more general education and special education teachers have been assigned to co-teach in classrooms of students with and without disabilities. Although the general education and special education teacher both have knowledge of teaching, they may not have experience in working so closely with another teacher—even if they've been teaching for years! So, now that you are going to be a co-teacher, what do you need to know to be successful? Or, if you've been co-teaching, what do you want to know to strengthen your partnership?

The purpose of this book is to address both teachers in the partnership. Each co-teacher is encouraged to recognize the differing perspectives of his or her partner. Chapters in the book provide an overview of good teaching practices in co-taught classrooms and practical advice regarding the relationship that both teachers can easily incorporate. This will provide a foundation for understanding the importance of co-teaching in the context of the current trend toward inclusion. The audience for this text is both co-teachers, with a focus on what each brings to the co-teaching relationship and how the strengths of each teacher can combine for the best student experiences and outcomes.

Throughout this book, five essential or guiding principles provide a framework for the co-teaching discussion. These essential principles are

- Respect perspectives
- Practice communication

- Focus on classroom teaching
- Build student success
- Improve and reflect on relationships

By practicing these principles, each co-teaching team will foster its own success. Each of these principles is discussed fully throughout the book. We encourage co-teaching pairs to share their thoughts and insights about these principles with each other.

Most teachers entering co-teaching roles feel that they know how to instruct their students and how to teach their classes. So why is this book dedicated to the idea that two teachers need to learn how to co-teach? Simply, successful co-teaching does not "just happen." It requires more from teachers than merely having knowledge of instruction and curriculum. Both teachers must find common ground and develop an ability to work together in their teaching. Some have stated that co-teaching is like a professional marriage (Friend & Cook, 2007). Think of all of the complexities of teaching (curriculum, classroom routines) combined with the intricacies of marriage (communication, trust), and it becomes apparent that both co-teaching partners could use a little advice.

To help co-teachers and potential co-teachers gain the most useful information, each chapter includes 1) examples of things to do in your classroom and of ways to work with your co-teacher, 2) suggestions of conversations to have with your co-teacher and of ways to enhance your co-teaching, and 3) Reflections and Connections sections. The Reflections and Connections prompts are designed to help teachers reflect on their individual co-teaching experience and to connect the reading to their co-teaching practices. We suggest that the reader begin a co-teaching journal and spend time reflecting on each of the questions in the Reflections section of each chapter. Reflection will help you understand your own perspective better, and creating a journal of these reflections provides a good resource for discussing with your co-teacher how your classroom and relationship will operate. For experienced or beginning co-teachers, the Connections questions and prompts should be completed with your current co-teaching situation in mind. Prospective co-teachers should think about their future co-taught classrooms.

On the accompanying DVD, the reader will find both templates for useful documents (progress monitoring forms, lesson plans) and video clips that support the content of each chapter. The co-teachers and administrator in the video clips are actual co-teachers and an administrator demonstrating or discussing their partnership. The purpose of the DVD is to provide further exploration of the challenges and benefits of co-teaching that supports the chapter discussions. What's on the DVD? and What Should I Watch for on the DVD? sections at the beginning of chapters provide guidance for getting the most out of the DVD. There is also a DVD Guide at the back of the book.

Both the book and the DVD can be used in a linear, chapter-by-chapter format or by selecting specific topics to explore. Both teachers are encouraged to compose reflections on their co-teaching as they read the book or navigate the DVD. Each co-teaching team is unique, as are the needs of the team. The Reader's Guide at the end of the book helps teams make additional connections between the content of the book and real-life experiences.

Co-teaching can be an exciting adventure for both teachers; however, when there are unresolved difficulties or there is a lack of commitment to the partnership, it can become a dismal experience to be endured. Whereas a poor partnership can be uncomfortable for the co-teachers, it is even more difficult for their students. Ultimately, both co-teachers need to focus their energy and passion on the success of their students. The mandate to foster success for all students in the classroom has made co-teaching more prevalent. That is the overarching reason that two co-teachers need to know how to co-teach together: student success!

# Respect
# Perspectives

# 1

# The Basics
# of Co-Teaching

## CHAPTER CHECKLIST

Once you have read this chapter, you should be able to

○ Describe the six models of co-teaching.
○ Identify which model(s) of co-teaching might be the best model for you and your co-teacher.
○ Identify the characteristics of successful co-teaching.
○ Discuss the research related to co-teaching effectiveness.

 *WHAT'S ON THE DVD?*

This is a sample co-taught lesson that follows the Team Teaching format.

 *WHAT SHOULD I WATCH FOR ON THE DVD?*

• Can you determine which teacher is the content expert? Why or why not?
• What do these teachers do that helps them present themselves to the class as a team?

In recent years, there has been a trend in education toward expanded use of inclusive classrooms. Beyond the work of advocates and researchers, this trend has been accelerated by legislation (Individuals with Disabilities Education Improvement Act [IDEA] of 2004 [PL 108-446]) that focuses on students with disabilities being served in the least restrictive environment. In special education, there is a "continuum of service" that describes the various placements or settings in which educational services for students with disabilities can be provided (Mastropieri & Scruggs, 2010). The placement that allows students the greatest opportunity to receive services with their peers without disabilities is within the general education classroom; this is generally considered the least restrictive placement option, though this placement will not be appropriate for every child.

Concurrently there has been an increase in the use of co-teaching as a strategy to facilitate inclusion in general education classrooms (Friend & Cook, 2007). The purpose of this strategy is to help focus instruction for all of the students in an inclusive classroom by combining the strengths of a general education teacher and a special education teacher. The general education teacher is knowledgeable in the content of the curriculum, whereas the special education teacher is knowledgeable about specific instructional strategies that may assist students both with and without disabilities. Other combinations of professionals may also engage in co-teaching, such as a special education teacher paired with a speech therapist to provide a language-rich classroom experience or two general education teachers co-teaching and combining their instructional and content knowledge to benefit all of their students (e.g., a history teacher and an English teacher joining classes to co-teach a unit on *Animal Farm* [Orwell, 1993] and the Russian Revolution). However, the majority of co-teaching pairs consist of a general education and a special education teacher.

The models of instruction teachers use in inclusive teaching are described as 1) the *consultant model,* where the general education teacher "consults" the special education teacher for guidance on modifications, assessments, and remediation; 2) the *coaching model,* where each teacher provides "coaching" in his or her area of expertise; and 3) the *co-teaching model,* where the two teachers provide instruction together in a classroom (Austin, 2001). Friend and Cook stated, "Co-teaching involves at least two appropriately credentialed professionals," and further described the importance of these individuals viewing each other as instructional and professionals equals, where one is not dominant over the other, for co-teaching to be successful (2007, p. 114). Although the various models of instruction for inclusive teaching are all valuable, this book focuses on the co-teaching model, specifically with two peers defined as a general education teacher and a special education teacher.

## MODELS OF CO-TEACHING

Once teachers or administrators decide that a collaborative relationship will take the form of co-teaching, the teachers need to consider the six models that their co-teaching can take. The co-teaching models include the following:

1. One Teach, One Observe
2. One Teach, One Assist
3. Station Teaching
4. Parallel Teaching
5. Alternative Teaching
6. Team Teaching

Friend and Cook (2007) stressed the importance of both teachers understanding how to implement the models in their classroom. It is also important to understand that each teacher in the partnership must feel comfortable with the model chosen for the classroom. One of the first discussions a prospective pair of co-teachers should have is, "How do we want to teach together?" Table 1.1 presents an overview of the models of co-teaching and their potential benefits and challenges.

Each of the models of co-teaching has specific characteristics, and there are also distinctions based on the school setting (elementary, middle, and high). In an early elementary classroom, it is common to have the room arranged into "centers" that may provide a focus for a Station Teaching model. In a middle school classroom, it may be easiest to divide the students into two groups to allow teachers to work with fewer students. This would support the Parallel Teaching model. In a high school classroom, there may be a need for one of the teachers to move around the room assisting individual or small groups of students, resulting in a One Teach, One Assist model. This may be an easier model to implement when one of the teachers lacks specific content knowledge. In all school settings, each of the models may be effective as long as both teachers are committed to a successful partnership.

The model that suits a co-teaching pair may also vary depending on how comfortable the teachers are with working and planning together, how much co-planning time they have, how comfortable they each are with the content, and logistics such as the size of the classroom. Team Teaching requires a more coordinated approach, with both teachers having a firm grasp of the content and spending time to work out the details of who will be doing what. Alternatively, if co-planning time is limited, perhaps the co-teachers will split up units and each take the lead on different units, or perhaps they will each take a topic and do Station Teaching, wherein they each plan their own station without needing as much coordinated co-planning time. If the special educator is less comfortable with the content, the team may find that it is best for that co-teacher to take a less active role in initial

**Table 1.1.** Models of co-teaching

| Model of co-teaching | Description | Pros | Cons |
|---|---|---|---|
| One Teach, One Observe | One teacher teaches the lesson while the other teacher observes students. The observer may be collecting data on an individual student, small group of students, or the entire class. It is vital that teachers take turns being the observer and the teacher to balance the responsibilities. | The collection of data may assist future planning and instruction. | The teacher collecting the data may not be seen as a teacher by the students. |
| One Teach, One Assist | One teacher teaches the lesson while the other teacher moves around the classroom providing individual and small-group assistance to students. Again, it is vital that teachers take turns being the assisting teacher so that neither is seen as "just" an assistant. | The teacher who is "drifting" around the classroom can provide individual and small-group assistance. | The "drifting" teacher may be seen as an assistant and not an equal teacher. |
| Station Teaching | Each teacher teaches part of the lesson. The classroom is set up in centers or "stations" that students rotate through. Each teacher is responsible for delivering instruction concurrently. | Each teacher is responsible for planning and teaching a portion of a lesson.<br>Both teachers are seen as teachers by the students. | The physical layout of the classroom must be considered.<br>Classroom noise levels may rise. |
| Parallel Teaching | Each teacher teaches the lesson to a small number of students. Typically, the classroom is divided into two sections. Each teacher has a section to teach. | This model helps to lower the teacher-to-student ratio; however, both teachers must know the content of the lesson. | The lesson needs to end at approximately the same time (teacher pacing).<br>Classroom noise levels may rise. |
| Alternative Teaching | Each teacher may pull aside small groups of students for specific instruction. It may be for enhancement, remedial, review, or even social skills. | This model encourages small-group instruction.<br>Students may get more individual time with a teacher. | The group members must vary.<br>It may take more teacher planning time to assign group membership. |
| Team Teaching | Both teachers are responsible for planning and conducting the instruction. They work together as a team. | Both teachers deliver instruction.<br>Both teachers move around the classroom. | Students are shared between the teachers.<br>Teachers must establish both mutual trust and respect for this model to be successful. |

instruction until he or she becomes more fluent in the content. We suggest that the team find a way to make even less content-savvy teachers the instructional lead for some part of the class (i.e., review, homework overview) to keep students aware that both teachers are equal in the classroom. Finally, sometimes logistics will dictate which models of co-teaching are practical. For instance, if classroom space is limited, it may not be possible to successfully implement Station Teaching or Parallel Teaching.

Deciding on which model of co-teaching to implement should be a mutual teacher decision; however, teachers may decide to vary the model based on the content to be taught on a given day and their comfort level with each other, and the choice of model may change over time. One teacher partnership may begin co-teaching by implementing a One Teach, One Assist model, then move to Station Teaching, and finally settle on a Team Teaching approach. Another pair of teachers may decide that Team Teaching suits the content and the teachers' comfort level with each other. Whether co-teaching is assigned by an administrator or chosen by the pair of teachers, the co-teachers need to have a discussion and mutually agree on which model they are most comfortable using as they begin teaching together.

## RESEARCH ON CO-TEACHING

Given the increased use of co-teaching in inclusive classrooms, it is distressing to realize that there is only a small amount of research on this topic. In 2001, Murawski and Swanson conducted a meta-analysis of research articles in which 89 articles related to co-teaching were identified; however, only 6 articles contained sufficient information for quantitative analysis. The meta-analysis was focused on the efficacy of co-teaching in classrooms, and the authors were able to calculate effect sizes for several variables, including dependent measures such as grades, math and reading achievement, and social and attitudinal outcomes. However, no more than 3 studies considered any one of the variables, making the effect sizes inconclusive. The conclusion of the meta-analysis was that more research on co-teaching was needed (Murawski & Swanson, 2001). See Box 1.1 for a description of *meta-analysis.*

In 2007, Scruggs, Mastropieri, and McDuffie conducted a metasynthesis of qualitative research on co-teaching. These researchers identified 32 studies relating to co-teaching in inclusive classrooms and utilized qualitative research methods such as teacher interviews and surveys. The focus of the metasynthesis was to identify broader themes related to co-teaching based on individual studies. This metasynthesis identified several common concerns regarding co-teaching: the need for co-planning time, the importance of administrative support for co-teaching, and that the most commonly used model of co-teaching was One Teach, One Assist (Scruggs et al., 2007). Concerns relating to the relationship between the two teachers were also identified. Unfortunately, these concerns related to the special education teacher providing more assistance than teaching. The special education

---

**BOX** $1.1$ **Defined: meta-analysis and metasynthesis**

### META-ANALYSIS

A meta-analysis is a large study that combines data from primary source studies that include numerical, or quantitative, data in their results. When evaluating interventions, readers should give more weight to a meta-analysis than to individual studies because it combines, in an objective manner, the results of many studies, increasing the size and diversity of the sample.

Results are in the format of *effect size*, a number that provides an objective "strength" of the intervention. Lloyd, Forness, and Kavale (1998) provided a good discussion on effect sizes.

### METASYNTHESIS

A metasynthesis is a large study that combines nonnumerical, qualitative data from primary source studies. When evaluating interventions, readers should give more weight to a metasynthesis than to individual studies because it combines, in an objective manner, the results of many studies, increasing the size and diversity of the sample.

Results are in the format of trends and themes from the original research studies. Krathwohl (2009) provided a good discussion of qualitative methods.

*Note:* Quantitative analysis focuses on *quantifying* (numerically) data. Qualitative analysis focuses on the attributes *(qualities)* or explanations of data.

---

teacher was also noted to infrequently utilize instructional strategies (peer tutoring, cognitive strategy instruction, mnemonics) known to be effective (Scruggs et al., 2007). The conclusion of this metasynthesis is also that more research on co-teaching is needed. See Box 1.1 for a description of *metasynthesis*. Research since 2007 has focused on co-teaching combined with other interventions, or on what makes good co-teaching relationships, and not on the effects of co-teaching on students' academic achievement. We address these other areas of research in later chapters.

Despite the conclusions that more research is needed, there are indications that co-teaching as a strategy has potential benefits for inclusive classrooms. In 2001, Austin conducted a survey of co-teachers regarding their perceptions of co-teaching. Although the number of returned surveys (139) is relatively small, the participants' responses revealed that co-teachers needed feedback from each other, co-planning time, and time to develop their relationship; the survey also reflected the need for administrative support (Austin, 2001). These findings are relatively consistent with other research; however, there was an unexpected result within the participants' responses. Austin found "that a majority of the co-teachers surveyed and interviewed had not volunteered for the experience and yet a major percentage indicated that they considered co-teaching worthwhile" (2001, p. 252).

---

**BOX 1.2 Co-teaching benefits and challenges for teachers**

**BENEFITS**

Research indicates that co-teachers are generally positive about co-teaching. The benefits reported include

- A lower student-to-teacher ratio
- Shared responsibilities: attendance taking, material preparation, grading, and classroom management
- Mutual support
- Opportunities to share expertise: General education teachers have specific content or discipline knowledge, whereas special education teachers have strategies and methods to assist student learning.

**CHALLENGES**

Research also indicates that co-teachers recognize that there are certain things they need to have a successful co-teaching experience and that it is sometimes a challenge to get what they need. Teachers recognize that they need

- Co-planning time
- Training in co-teaching techniques
- Time to build the co-teaching relationship
- Administrative support

*Sources:* Austin (2001); Scruggs et al. (2007).

---

Even co-teachers who are assigned (rather than volunteer) to co-teach may find the reality of teaching with another person to be a positive experience. The previously discussed metasynthesis also noted a finding that co-teachers reported mostly positive attitudes about co-teaching (Scruggs et al., 2007). These positive attitudes toward co-teaching may be related to a reduced student-to-teacher ratio, sharing of teaching responsibilities (grading, attendance taking), and support for each other. Box 1.2 highlights the benefits of co-teaching and also the challenges co-teaching presents for teachers.

Although the co-teachers may have a positive attitude toward working together, there seems to be a lack of evidence to support the efficacy of co-teaching relating to academic achievement or student grades. In both the metasynthesis and the survey study, co-teachers reported positive student outcomes in terms of academic achievement (Austin, 2001; Scruggs et al., 2007); however, there is little empirical or statistical evidence that supports this belief (Murawski & Swanson, 2001). There nevertheless can be many benefits of co-teaching for students, and these are described in Box 1.3.

---

**BOX 1.3** | **Co-teaching benefits for students**

Research on co-teaching and academic achievement is limited, and there is little evidence of the effectiveness of co-teaching on academic achievement. The research does indicate that co-taught classes have a lower student-to-teacher ratio, which may promote student achievement (Lloyd et al., 1998; Magiera & Zigmond, 2005).

One of the reasons for the trend toward inclusive classrooms is that students with disabilities benefit from social interaction with their peers without disabilities (Mastropieri & Scruggs, 2010). Co-teaching provides supports for students with disabilities within the general education classroom and thus facilitates inclusive education. The special education teacher can assist all of the students but is trained in strategies and techniques to assist the students with special needs to successfully participate with their peers.

---

## CONCLUSION

As you read through this chapter, you should have gained an overview of the use of co-teaching in inclusive classrooms, the models of co-teaching, and the research (or lack thereof) on co-teaching. The current trend toward co-teaching is likely to continue as teachers increasingly are being asked to work together to provide instruction for all students.

Having learned some of the basics of co-teaching, can you now identify a model of co-teaching that might work for you and your teaching partner? Can you describe how co-teaching might look in your classroom? If you are a general education teacher, can you identify some of the possible benefits of co-teaching? If you are a special education teacher, can you identify some of the concerns related to co-teaching?

Whether you are an experienced co-teacher or a new co-teacher, the experience can be exciting, challenging, and worthwhile. If venturing into this new territory feels as though you have "fallen off a cliff" in the classroom, keep in mind that one of the gifts of co-teaching is that you are not alone—your teaching partner has also fallen off that cliff. The chapters that follow provide ideas and strategies to help you gain your footing. We encourage you also to try to consider other perspectives and incorporate your own ideas as you read through the book. By combining the suggestions in this book with your own teaching style, you can make your own co-teaching relationship stronger and uniquely your own.

Welcome to the adventure of co-teaching!

 ***REFLECTIONS***

---

• What is your comfort level with the different roles in each of the co-teaching models?

 **CONNECTIONS**

Experienced co-teachers

- What benefits of co-teaching have you seen for yourself as a co-teacher? For your students?
- Which models of co-teaching do you use? Which other models might you consider?

Beginning co-teachers

- Which models of co-teaching are you currently using?
- Experiment with other models by setting a goal to use a different model at least once a month.

Prospective co-teachers

- What are your general feelings about co-teaching? Are you excited? Nervous?
- What about co-teaching energizes you most?

# What Each
# Teacher Brings

---

**CHAPTER CHECKLIST**

Once you have read this chapter, you should be able to

○  Identify the state or national standards that will be addressed in your co-taught classroom.

○  Describe how the No Child Left Behind Act of 2001 (NCLB; PL 107-110) and high-stakes testing affect your teaching responsibilities in a co-taught classroom.

○  Discuss each student's individualized education program (IEP) with your co-teacher and decide who will be responsible for which accommodations and how you will incorporate and address goals into instructional time.

○  Identify the purpose of special education for the students with disabilities in your classroom.

○  List specific concerns that a general education teacher may have related to including learners with special needs in the general education curriculum.

---

 *WHAT'S ON THE DVD?*

Sherry, a general educator, talks about how her co-teacher, Craig, helps her teach more effectively—offering rewording for immediate clarification, different ways of thinking, and additional approaches that make concepts more accessible by presenting several angles.

 **WHAT SHOULD I WATCH FOR ON THE DVD?**

- How do these co-teachers' strengths play together to benefit their students?
- What kinds of ideas and input do you think a co-teacher can bring to your classroom to improve instruction?

## GENERAL EDUCATION TEACHER OVERVIEW

The general education teacher is responsible for planning and teaching the subject content (e.g., science, math, reading, history). The curriculum is varied for each content area and addresses what information was previously covered, what information will be needed as a foundation for future learning, how state or national standards will be addressed, and how instruction will be sequenced (Hunkins & Ornstein, 2009). Most general education teachers had specific coursework during their preservice teacher education relating to curriculum and the methods to teach specific content.

Since the early 1990s, there has been a focus on testing students' content knowledge (i.e., using standardized tests) as a way to measure effective teaching and hold teachers accountable for student outcomes. Since the passage of NCLB in 2001, high-stakes testing has become a significant factor in how general education teachers must structure their lessons and plan their instruction. This focus on high-stakes testing has become so prevalent that students with disabilities included in general education classes are being required to take end-of-course assessments in larger numbers than prior to 2001. In fact, IDEA of 2004 mandates that an IEP must address whether a student with special needs will take the standardized test—and, if so, what testing modifications may be used—and NCLB also limits the percentage of students with disabilities who can be exempt from these assessments.

This focus on testing as a measure of teacher effectiveness has become a concern for general educators. In many schools, teacher performance evaluations are being linked to how well students perform on these tests (Protheroe, 2001). In 2010, numerous news reports (both print and television) focused on the nationwide discussion of tying teacher merit pay to student performance on high-stakes tests. So, student performance on standardized tests is an important consideration in planning how (and what) the general educator must teach.

The general education teacher must juggle multiple responsibilities, such as following the scope and sequence of the curriculum, thoroughly understanding the teaching of specific content, focusing lessons on state or national standards, and ensuring that all of the students are prepared to pass standards-based examinations. These responsibilities and accompanying concerns must be addressed to ensure a harmonious co-teaching relationship. The special education teacher needs to understand how these responsibilities inform the teaching perspective of the general educator.

## SPECIAL EDUCATION TEACHER OVERVIEW

To understand the role of the special education teacher in the co-teaching classroom, the co-teaching team needs to have a similar understanding of the purpose of special education. The purpose of education is a much-argued point, and the purpose of special education, specifically, has no wider consensus. At the most basic level, special education law dictates that the purpose of special education is to provide to all students with disabilities a free appropriate public education that will prepare them for adulthood in the areas of education, employment, and independent living (IDEA 2004). However, the matters of how to provide a free appropriate public education and what the outcomes should be are areas of contention in the field.

NCLB and the 2004 reauthorization of IDEA combined to provide motivation to serve more students with disabilities in the general education classroom, because more students with disabilities were being held to the same academic standard as their peers without disabilities than ever before. As students with disabilities move out of resource or self-contained classrooms and into the general education classroom, the legal purpose of special education has not changed, but the methods by which special educators fulfill that purpose *has* changed, and co-teaching has become more prevalent.

As the laws took effect and the methods of instructional delivery changed across the country, special educators and general educators were faced with redefining their roles in their classrooms. As stated previously in this chapter, the general education teacher brings to the relationship deep and thorough content knowledge. Though many special educators do have content knowledge, unless they are the teacher of record for a student in a self-contained classroom, they do not have to hold any content certification to teach. Rather, state special education licenses require knowledge of the constructs of and interventions related to disabilities. Some states want special educators to be eligible for a license in a content area as well as in special education, but many do not (Education Commission of the States, 2007).

So, then, what is the role of the special educator in the co-teaching relationship? By training, special educators are focused on individual needs, goals, and gains, fine tuning instruction for each individual to meet his or her specific needs. Another strength for special educators, due to the nature of the population with which they are trained to work, is behavior management.

## CONTENT KNOWLEDGE

Although the general educator must have content-specific knowledge, there are distinctions between the knowledge needed to teach and the qualifications required at the elementary and secondary levels. The instructional focus of early elementary curriculum is related to the teaching of reading and math, though other content areas (e.g., science, arts, and social studies) are addressed. Many general education teachers studied in college to become teachers with majors such as elementary education or education. The coursework required for these majors is often focused on the methods and curriculum for teaching at the elementary level. So, many elementary-level general educators studied and trained for the specific curriculum they are teaching.

At the secondary level, general education teachers often specialize in specific content and earned a college degree in this field (e.g., chemistry, English). The U.S. Department of Education's National Center for Education Statistics reported that "more than three-quarters of teachers with a main assignment in English (84 percent), science (87 percent), and social science (84 percent) held a major in the respective field" (2008, p. 17). At the same time, the report found that only 62% of math teachers held a degree in mathematics (U.S. Department of Education, 2008). So, many secondary-level general educators studied content areas in depth for the curriculum they teach.

In addition, NCLB has specific language related to "highly qualified teacher" that also emphasizes the importance of teachers having specific content knowledge. Although the definition of *highly qualified* seems to vary depending on an individual state's requirements, more school districts are reviewing college transcripts to ensure that teachers have credit hours in specific content. In fact, more states are having teachers take standardized examinations (e.g., PRAXIS II Subject Assessments) to ensure that teachers meet content knowledge standards.

Given general education teachers' qualifications, education, and focus on meeting standards, it is easy to understand their occasional reluctance to share these teaching responsibilities with special education teachers (Friend & Cook, 2007). This reluctance must be reduced for an effective co-teaching relationship to evolve. The general educator in a co-teaching relationship can benefit from the experience of the special educator with effective instructional strategies.

### National and State Standards

Most content areas have a national organization that has established standards (e.g., National Science Teachers Association, 1996). Some states have established their own standards (e.g., Virginia Department of Education's [2003] Standards of Learning) that the general education teacher must consider. The U.S. Department of Education (2010) has also encouraged adoption of national standards called the Common Core in its grant program to support school reform efforts, known as Race to the Top. These standards may also inform the high-stakes tests that students must take to ensure adequate yearly progress, which is being used as a measure of school effectiveness under NCLB guidelines.

Generally, most content experts agree that the standards reflect what knowledge a student should have of specific material. There may be some variability in what is taught at each grade level, but the broader view of the discipline is reflected in the standards. These standards inform the curriculum that will be taught in the classroom. They are also the standards that will be measured by the high-stakes tests that students will take. See Box 2.1 for specific examples of standards.

For a successful co-teaching relationship, both teachers need to have an understanding of what specific standards they need to address in their lessons. This discussion should occur prior to the school year so that planning

---

**BOX 2.1  Sample standards**

The following are examples of science standards related to physical science (matter).

An elementary science standard (Grade 5) from the Virginia Department of Education (2003) *Standards of Learning* states the following:

> 5.4 The student will investigate and understand that matter is anything that has mass, takes up space, and occurs as a solid, liquid, or gas. Key concepts include:
>
> a.  atoms, elements, molecules, and compounds;
> b.  mixtures including solutions; and
> c.  the effect of heat on the states of matter. (p. 17)

A secondary science standard (Grades 9–12) from the National Science Teachers Association (1996) states the following:

> The student will investigate and understand the following concepts related to matter:
>
> a.  Structure of atoms
> b.  Structure and properties of matter
> c.  Chemical reactions
> d.  Motions and forces
> e.  Conservation of energy and increase in disorder
> f.  Interactions of energy and matter. (p. 106)

Clearly, the content is related, and the state standard reflects the national standard. The standards are developmentally appropriate to the grade level of the students. The elementary physics standard is related to understanding the concept of mass, whereas the secondary standard provides for a more in-depth understanding of the concept of matter.

---

**BOX 2.2** | **Tips for co-teachers**

The special education teacher may be assigned to co-teach more than one grade level or content area, making it difficult to manage all of the standards that will need to be addressed. It may be helpful to review the standards at the start of the school year, prior to planning meetings with the general education teacher. This will help to familiarize the special education teacher with the general outline of the standards and provide background knowledge prior to the joint planning meeting.

The general education teacher may have been teaching this specific grade level and content area for more than a year. There may be concepts or skills that have been difficult for students in the past. For example, in previous years, students may have lacked the mathematical skills to calculate the equation for distance and speed in a physics class or confused the definitions of *homonyms* and *antonyms* in a language arts class. The general education teacher should identify these areas of concern prior to the start of the school year. This will help to identify areas that could be addressed by the special education teacher at the joint planning meeting.

---

for the standards can be done concurrently with planning for teaching the curriculum. See Box 2.2 for tips for co-teachers.

## Scope and Sequence of Curriculum

The general educator has an understanding of what should have been previously taught, what will be taught in the future, and how the specific lessons fit into the broader scope of content (Hunkins & Ornstein, 2009). As standards-based testing has become more prevalent, individual school districts and states have focused on standardizing the curriculum, adding to the teacher's innate and learned knowledge about curriculum sequencing (Protheroe, 2001). In many school districts, there is a plan for what should be taught and when during the school year it should be taught for each grade level (elementary) or content area (secondary). There are various labels for this "master plan," but it is the scope (what will be taught) and sequence (in what order it will be taught) of the curriculum. The general education teacher is responsible for structuring the units and lessons to align with the scope and sequence of the curriculum.

In a successful co-teaching relationship, both teachers should be familiar with the subject's scope and sequence. Many curriculum guides are available from district or state web sites and should be reviewed by both teachers prior to the initial planning meeting at the start of the school year.

## Statewide or Districtwide Assessments

As previously noted, there has been an increased focus on statewide or districtwide assessments to measure academic achievement. In a co-taught class (inclusion), the general education teacher may have concerns about the academic achievement of learners with disabilities. In recent years there has been a push to include learners with disabilities in these statewide assessments to ensure accountability for all students regardless of disability. The National Assessment of Educational Progress data suggest that students with disabilities are being included in the same assessments as their peers without disabilities while receiving the bulk of their education in the general education classroom (Kitmitto & Bandeira, 2008). This increased accountability for teaching a group of students who, until the mid-2000s, were included less frequently in high-stakes assessments is another consideration for general educators as they plan and teach. See Box 2.3 for a discussion of NCLB and assessment.

Often, learners with disabilities struggle with the format and time pressure of tests and may have testing accommodations listed on their IEPs. The special education teacher must ensure that the accommodations are provided for testing and must assist learners with disabilities in increasing their test-taking abilities. In fact, a special education teacher may teach specific test-taking strategies that will benefit all of the students in the class. (See

---

**BOX 2.3** **The No Child Left Behind Act of 2001 (NCLB; PL 107-110) and assessment**

NCLB details specific requirements for the assessments that will be used to evaluate academic progress. These requirements for assessments used by states, as stated in NCLB, must include the following:

1. Be the same academic assessments used to measure the achievement of all children.
2. Be aligned with the State's challenging academic content and student academic achievement standards, and provide coherent information about student attainment of such standards.
3. Be used for purposes for which such assessments are valid and reliable and be consistent with relevant, nationally, recognized professional and technical standards. (Sec. 1111 [3][C][i–iii])

In addition, the legislation addresses the importance of including learners with special needs in the assessments. It states,

> The reasonable adaptations and accommodations for students with disabilities (as defined under section 602(3) of the Individuals with Disabilities Education Act) as necessary to measure the academic achievement of such students relative to State academic content and State student academic achievement standards should be done. (Sec. 1111 [3][C][viii][II])

The law reminds educators that they must provide "reasonable adaptations and accommodations for students with disabilities" (Sec. 1111 [3][C][viii][II]) on the state academic assessments. If an individualized education program (IEP) team decides that a student will not be taking the state assessments, parents must sign off on the decision.

The importance of high-stakes assessments as a measure of accountability for both schools and general education teachers must be recognized as a serious ongoing concern for both co-teachers.

Chapter 7 for an expanded discussion of assessment and Chapter 11 for test-taking strategies.)

## SPECIAL EDUCATION'S FOCUS ON THE INDIVIDUAL STUDENT

One of the key reasons that co-teaching exists, as discussed in Chapter 1, is because students with disabilities are spending more time in general education classrooms than ever before (Kauffman & Hallahan, 2005). However, placement in the general education classroom does not eliminate the requirement for the school to provide specialized instruction to meet the needs of students with disabilities. The fundamental activity of special education is to provide instruction and services that vary in some way from the standard or typical instruction occurring in a classroom (Kauffman & Hallahan, 2005). In a co-teaching relationship, it is the special education teacher's duty to make sure that instruction is addressing individual students' IEP goals so that students with disabilities are receiving their special education.

Just as the general education teacher has multiple responsibilities, special education teachers have responsibilities that affect their perspective in the classroom, and it is helpful for the general education teacher to understand a little about these. Special educators have caseloads that often contain students in multiple classrooms, requiring them to work with multiple general educators; they must collect data and complete paperwork for reporting on the progress of students with disabilities related to county and state academic standards and also to IEP goals; they must ensure that the legally binding IEP is being implemented appropriately, including classroom and testing accommodations; and they must alter instruction and the classroom environment to ensure that a student's disability is not impeding his or her ability to demonstrate learning. In addition, special education teachers, like general education teachers, have multiple responsibilities related to students with IEPs: developing the IEP, managing the IEP meeting, and communicating with parents about their student.

### Differentiation and Remediation

Special educators are well equipped to be champions for both differentiation and remediation of instruction. Because the focus in special education is on the individual, it is a special educator's strength to assess and address individual needs. Often a resource room or a self-contained classroom is like a three-ring circus, with multiple students working on many different levels and subjects. It is a skill to be able to balance a variety of levels working at one time, a skill that special educators have been trained and prepared for since the inception of special education. Remediation is another area in which special education teachers have expertise. Though students with some disabilities have worked at grade level in the past, that was the exception rather than the rule (Hallahan, Lloyd, Kauffman, Weiss, & Martinez, 2005; Kauffman, 2005). That means that anyone teaching to the individual needs of students with disabilities was remediating instruction. Special education teachers bring to the co-teaching team knowledge and experience in meeting the needs of all learners by teaching in a variety of ways using research-based instructional strategies (see Chapters 10 and 11).

## Individualized Education Programs

The most important document for any student with a disability is his or her IEP. Though each reauthorization of IDEA is a reminder that students with disabilities are required to have access to and be working on, to the extent possible, the general education curriculum, it is the IEP that lays out the plan for how to make that happen. The IEP is, technically, developed by a team including the student (when appropriate), a general education teacher, a special education teacher, an administrator, and other related service personnel (Bateman & Linden, 2006). However, the special education teacher is typically the person at the table most knowledgeable about the legal requirements of special education and the possibilities that exist because of a student's identified disability and generally provides a draft of the completed document for the team to review, revise, and approve. So, though both the general education and special education teachers sit at the table when the document is written and approved, it is not uncommon for the special education teacher to take responsibility for making sure that the team follows the IEP, a legally binding document.

IEPs contain a number of parts, many of which are not relevant to our discussion. The most relevant parts are goals, modifications, and accommodations. The *goals* section of an IEP lays out what each student with a disability is working on, in addition to or instead of the general education curriculum (Bateman & Linden, 2006). For instance, a middle school student who is several grade levels below in math may have specific goals related to memorization of math facts but would not have goals related to social studies because he or she is expected to be on grade level for that area. Though the general education teacher needs to be aware of and attend to these goals, in a co-teaching environment the special education teacher can take instructional responsibility and differentiate instruction for this student so that he or she is working to meet IEP goals.

The term *modification* is almost always used in tandem with the term *accommodation*, but they really are different (see Box 2.4). A modification is a variance away from the general education curriculum. For instance, it is not appropriate for a student with a severe intellectual disability who cannot read to be working at all on the grade-level curriculum in high school. The IEP team may decide on an alternate curriculum and will specify the modification, or major change to content, in the IEP (Bateman & Linden, 2006). If there are modifications to the curriculum, students will still be assessed to hold schools accountable for progress, as discussed in the earlier section on NCLB; however, they will be assessed in an alternate format.

---

**BOX** **2.4** | **Defined: accommodations and modifications**

---

### ACCOMMODATIONS

Accomodations are small changes that provide access to the same resource the general education students are using. They do *not* alter curriculum. Some examples include changes in timing, presentation, format, setting, and availability of aides.

### MODIFICATIONS

Modifications are changes to the curriculum standard that the student is responsible for, such as being able to describe Newton's Laws of Motion without being held responsible for calculating a velocity equation.

The specific format will vary depending on the state's requirements and the severity of the student's disability. See Chapter 7 for more information about assessing modified curricula.

Accommodations help students reach their goals and make the general education curriculum accessible. For example, a student who has a minor vision impairment may need an accommodation of large print. Legally, once written in the IEP, the teachers need to be sure that the student receives the large print accommodation. Either teacher can take responsibility for making the accommodation, and with this accommodation the student will be able to use materials to meet general education goals. Typically, because accommodations are more on the radar for the special education teacher, they become his or her responsibility in a co-teaching situation.

## The Individualized Education Program Team

The IEP team is comprised of the parents of the student, the student (when appropriate), a special education teacher, a general education teacher, and an administrator (principal or principal designee) (Bateman & Linden, 2006). The team can also include a guidance counselor, school psychologist, or related services professionals (speech-language clinician, physical therapist) or anyone else necessary to ensure that the student's educational needs will be met.

The purpose of the team is to develop an IEP that provides services to support the student's educational achievement. A special education teacher often functions as the case manager for students with disabilities. General education teachers also participate in the meeting to provide guidance on curriculum and classroom issues.

Each teacher within a co-teaching pair may participate in IEP teams and IEP development for different students. For example, a special education teacher may be assigned as case manager for a student not in any co-taught classes and the general education teacher he or she co-teaches with will not have a reason to be a part of that IEP team. In other cases, the general education co-teacher may participate on an IEP team with a special education teacher who is not his or her co-teacher even though the student is in their co-taught class. In some cases, both members of the team will participate in an IEP for a shared student. In all of these cases, both co-teachers must be prepared to participate by providing professional judgment and perspectives and also by bringing student work samples and data related to student academic or behavioral progress. It may be the case that co-teachers have a student with a disability in their class and neither teacher is regularly involved in that student's IEP team meetings. Regardless of how involved the team is in developing the IEP, the team must help the student work toward the goals outlined in the IEP, using the accommodations and modifications that the IEP team has agreed on.

A unique aspect of the IEP team is the requirement that parents (and students) participate in the meeting. This provides co-teachers an opportunity to establish a relationship with parents outside of the parent conference or grade reports. Co-teachers are encouraged to listen carefully to parental concerns, provide student work samples, and ensure that the needs of the student are addressed when writing the IEP.

## Behavior Management

Behavior management is a persistent concern for many teachers (Manning & Bucher, 2003), but as teachers gain experience, their class management systems become more established and consistent; more experienced teachers tend to have fewer behavior management issues (Mitchell & Arnold, 2004). However, due to the nature of disability—both with emotional and behavioral disabilities that may include overt behaviors and also with more academic disabilities that may result in communication or academic frustrations—students with disabilities tend to have more behavior problems than the general education population. Given that, even experienced general education teachers may need to rethink behavior management in the inclusive classroom (Hallahan, Kauffman, & Pullen, 2009). Special education teachers, especially those with endorsements in the area of emotional disturbance, have had training in behavior management that goes beyond everyday classroom management strategies. This advanced training may include employing applied behavior analysis, creating and implementing a behavior plan, and using positive behavior supports. These techniques are discussed more fully in Chapter 9.

Some of special educator's behavior management training will typically be relevant only if there is a student with severe emotional or behavioral disabilities in the class. Nonviolent crisis intervention (Crisis Prevention Institute, 2009), for instance, is a training program that many special educators go through that emphasizes de-escalation and preventive strategies to use with students at various points in the anger cycle. Specialized training such as this is certainly open to general educators but is more common in a special educator's repertoire because it is more pertinent to his or her long-term work.

In general, special education teachers tend to have more "tricks" in their behavior management bag due to their training. Behavioral interventions that a special education teacher develops are not impossible for a general educator teacher to develop and implement, but the special education teacher has more exposure to a variety of techniques (e.g., use of token economies, the Boys Town Model, social skills training, prize boxes). For instance, in the late 1970s and early 1980s, when special education at a national level was very young, research in the field largely focused on how to change student behaviors, mainly nonacademic (e.g., Bass, 1985; Rooney, Hallahan, & Lloyd, 1984; Rooney, Polloway, & Hallahan, 1985), but some academic as well (e.g., Goetz, Gee, & Sailor, 1985). In a search of the same article database for the same time period, there were very few articles related to behavior of students without disabilities.

In the co-teaching relationship, special educators tend to be the experts at handling challenging behavior. Knowledge of behavior management tools includes strategies for the large group, such as positive behavior support (see Chapter 9 for definition) and large group contingencies, but like so many other things special education teachers do, also extends to the individual level. Special education teachers are trained to gather data at individual levels and also to implement individual behavior management strategies such as self-monitoring, behavior contracts, and teaching appropriate skills and behaviors. Whereas the general education teacher concentrates on the whole class, the special education teacher can look at individuals' behaviors and address those needs.

## CONCLUSION

As you read through this chapter, it should be apparent that *both* teachers in a co-teaching team have significant but differing responsibilities, education, and experience. Each teacher has some requirements (standards, IEPs) that define his or her particular role within the classroom setting. The most

---

**BOX** **2.5**    **Resource book**

- **Book:** *Special Education: What It Is and Why We Need It*
- **Authors:** James M. Kauffman and Daniel P. Hallahan
- **Publisher:** Allyn & Bacon (2005)

This small, inexpensive book is an invaluable resource for any new teacher. It provides an excellent overview of the special education system and specific disabilities and addresses common concerns that teachers may have regarding teaching students with disabilities. It is a good read for any teacher, but co-teachers at any grade level will find it very useful.

successful team teachers appreciate and value the unique perspective that both team members contribute to their students. Box 2.5 describes a resource book that both teachers can review to enhance their knowledge of special education services. Both teachers are encouraged to read and discuss with each other their thoughts about special education.

Can you mark the items on the beginning of the chapter checklist as complete? If you are a general education teacher, do you have an understanding of the special education teacher's knowledge of IEPs, accommodations, modifications, and behavior management that can help you in your shared classroom? If you are the special education teacher, can you describe a curriculum standard for your students? Do you have an understanding of the importance of NCLB and high-stakes testing to the instruction provided by the general education teacher? Have you both gained an appreciation of how time consuming managing all of your responsibilities can be? It is hoped you have begun to develop a framework for succeeding as a classroom team.

 ### *REFLECTIONS*

- What do you bring to the table? In what areas are you an expert?
- What experiences or knowledge do you have in your co-teacher's area of expertise?

 ### *CONNECTIONS*

Experienced co-teachers

- How has working with your co-teacher made you more adept at his or her area of expertise?
- Even with your increased knowledge, what are you still most comfortable leaving in the hands of your co-teacher?

Beginning co-teachers

- How has each co-teacher brought his or her specific knowledge and skills to the table?

Prospective co-teachers

- How will you convey to your co-teacher what your expertise is?

# 3

# Becoming Co-Teachers

---

**CHAPTER CHECKLIST**

Once you have read this chapter, you should be able to

- List reasons why someone may volunteer to co-teach and why someone may be hesitant to volunteer.
- Talk with your co-teacher regarding how he or she feels about co-teaching together.

---

 **WHAT'S ON THE DVD?**

Sherry and Craig talk about how they began co-teaching, their shared philosophy, and planning practices.

 **WHAT SHOULD I WATCH FOR ON THE DVD?**

- What do these co-teachers do that makes them successful?
- How can I talk with my co-teacher about working toward a shared philosophy for our classroom?

## VOLUNTEER CO-TEACHERS

Change is hard, but when individuals have a say in the change and have chosen to create the change, it is often a little easier and more likely to be successful. It is a big change to have been a single teacher in the classroom with complete control over the classroom rules, details, and policies and then shift to a collaborative co-teaching setting in which two teachers are involved in decisions and instruction. When the two teachers about to engage in co-teaching have volunteered for the change, it is often easier because they are excited about the adventure and have some expectations about their new role, even as they experience apprehension about the change (Friend & Cook, 2007).

### The Paired Volunteer

Though it is common for teachers to pair up before approaching administrators about working together, there are instances where a general education or special education teacher may decide he or she wants to co-teach but does not have a specific partner picked out. If the school's administration has made it clear that more teachers will be co-teaching and asks for people who are willing, administrators may pair the teachers based on strengths, expertise, and scheduling needs. In addition, teachers may find that as a willing participant in co-teaching, they are paired with a new partner because their co-teacher moves or retires, or for administrative reasons. We do not recommend that, as common practice, administrators break up successful co-teaching teams, but sometimes the students' needs create a change in schedule that makes it no longer practical for two teachers to continue to co-teach together.

When two people have each volunteered to co-teach but then are paired by someone else to teach together, they will need more time to acclimate than will the pair who volunteer together. The teachers may have volunteered to co-teach for one of any number of reasons: excitement about collaborating with a colleague, the (inaccurate) idea that it would be "easier," prior positive experiences, realizing that many students with disabilities included in the general education classroom need support throughout the day and that this is one way to provide it, and seeking a change from the typical pattern of the school day. The motivation behind volunteering for the change is important because it shapes expectations. For instance, if a special education teacher wants to co-teach because she wants to better support students with disabilities and also provide support for struggling students without disabilities, she probably sees her role in the classroom as equal partner and expects to spend time co-planning with her general education counterpart. However, if the general education teacher's motivation to volunteer to co-teach is to seek a change in the typical school day, the special education teacher's vision of an equal partnership may not match the general education teacher's expectations.

If co-teachers have been paired by others, they will need to discuss their vision for the relationship. What models of co-teaching are each comfortable with? What is each teacher expecting to bring to the relationship? Why does each teacher want to co-teach? See Chapter 6 for topics all co-teachers will need to discuss as they prepare to co-teach.

## Volunteer Together

The smoothest transition and greatest success in co-teaching occurs when two people volunteer to co-teach together (McDuffie, 2010). Teachers typically decide to take the co-teaching "plunge" together because they have some knowledge of each other and think that they can work well together. They may be friends who are excited at the prospect of thinking through new challenges together. They may be co-workers who have shared students in the past and have come to respect each other's approach to instruction and student interaction. They may be two people who have struck up a conversation about co-teaching and decided they can make it work. It might even be that one of the teachers has an interest in co-teaching or predicts that the administration will soon require him or her to co-teach and so seeks out someone who seems to be a good match. See Box 3.1 for ideas of how to approach a potential co-teacher.

However they find each other, it is likely that the two teachers have, or will develop early on, a common understanding of co-teaching and a common philosophy about how their shared classroom will work. If they hatch the idea together, they probably have already talked about many of the first-year hang-ups (as discussed in Chapters 4, 5, and 9) and share a vision for the partnership. It will still take good communication and hard work to make the co-teaching experience successful, but enthusiasm will take this pair a long way, and the teachers will also have additional motivation to see this co-teaching relationship work; they are invested in the change and want to see a good outcome.

---

**BOX 3.1 Approaching a potential co-teacher**

- Look for someone who has demonstrated a willingness to try new things or has co-taught in the past. Flatter the person.
- Impress upon the person what you see as the benefits to co-teaching, both for the students and for you as teachers. Make him or her want this.
- Demonstrate that you will be wonderful to work with by giving some concrete examples of how this could work. Be excited!
- Avoid making the person feel attacked or put on the spot. Give him or her time to think about the idea and opportunities to say "no." Don't pressure.

---

**BOX** **3.2** **Why administrator support for co-teaching is essential**

- Administrators control the master schedule and can make it possible or impossible for co-teachers to have a common class as well as common planning time.
- Administrators are "the bosses," and it is imperative to keep them involved and have their support in changes to the job description.
- Administrators are evaluators, and evaluators provide the best feedback if they understand new initiatives.

---

A potential first hurdle for a new co-teaching team is the school administration. Two teachers who have a passion for co-teaching and have decided that they want to try co-teaching the following year will need to appeal to their administration to make it possible. The support of administrators is essential for the success of co-teaching (see Box 3.2 and Chapter 5), and if the practice of co-teaching is new to an administrator, it may take some convincing to get that critical support. Ideas for helping get an administrator to support a co-teaching endeavor include providing background information and research about co-teaching; presenting a well-envisioned plan for implementation; knowing what you are asking to co-teach, whether it is part of the school day, multiple class periods, or one subject or class (Rea & Connell, 2005a); and knowing what you need from the administrators for success, such as co-planning time, time to observe other co-teaching pairs, and ongoing professional development (McDuffie, 2010).

It is important to remember that just because two people have volunteered to co-teach, or even to co-teach together, that does not ensure a productive partnership. The pair will still need to work through any differences in purpose, roles, or philosophy that were brought into the relationship. Teachers will need to discuss their philosophies and policies related to grading and accepting late work, gum and food, allowing students to go to the water fountain or use the restroom, and general classroom rules (e.g., Do students need to raise their hands? Do they stand when they ask a question?). See Chapters 4, 5, and 9 for more information on some of these challenges and how to address them. If the teachers can keep coming back to their shared enthusiasm and the reason they wanted to embark upon this adventure, they will be able to solve their conflicts.

## AN ASSIGNED PARTNER

We would never encourage administrators to place teachers who are unwilling and unexcited about co-teaching into a partnership with another teacher; however, we recognize that assigned partnerships happen and need to be addressed. Perhaps "unwilling" is too strong a word. Probably the co-teachers are just apprehensive, just unknowledgeable about what this change will bring and how it will affect their daily lives. Almost certainly they will immediately bond with their new co-teacher and ride off into the sunset with a class full of high-achieving students trailing behind them. Or not.

The reality is that not every co-teacher wants to be a co-teacher, and not every teacher is a good co-teacher. Reasons for not volunteering to co-teach may include being overprotective of one's classroom space, not understanding co-teaching and what it involves, being afraid of letting someone see what you do and that it might not be perfect. However, even a nonvolunteer may be called upon to co-teach, so what do you do if the word comes down that you will be co-teaching this year?

First, recognize that one of the biggest keys to success in an inclusion classroom is a good working relationship between co-teachers (Mastropieri et al., 2005). What this means, if one or both partners did not choose to engage in the relationship, is that there may be some initial resentment, fear, and unease. It is important that the partners talk about their fears and expectations and work to get a common understanding of their new relationship. It is likely that if the pair did not choose this new role, one or both teachers may not be comfortable with what their counterpart does. The special education teacher may be concerned about being in a classroom with more students; the general education teacher may be concerned about teaching students with disabilities effectively. The more teachers talk about their concerns, the more able they are to have an effective relationship.

Most important, the co-teachers need to remember why they are in the classroom. Even if the co-teaching relationship is less than perfect, remember that co-teaching does not exist solely to bring two teachers together. Co-teaching exists to serve *students*. Co-teachers need to remember at all times that it is their job to make the situation work for the students. Even if the co-teachers are simply polite to each other outside of their shared classroom, they must demonstrate to their students their respect for each other. Co-teachers must present to the students a unified front, as though any personality or pedagogical conflicts do not exist, so as to provide the best education possible to their students. The co-teaching mantra needs to be, "whatever is best for the students."

## CONCLUSION

The relationship between co-teachers sets the tone for the class. It is important to recognize that co-teachers may be entering the relationship with different ideas and emotions. Co-teachers need to talk to each other about their expectations, fears, and excitement and work to come to common understandings of what their co-taught classroom will look like. Chapter 4 provides advice on how to work through these sometimes-difficult conversations.

**REFLECTIONS**

- Did you volunteer to co-teach, or were you directed to co-teach? How does that affect your expectations for co-teaching?
- What are your expectations for this partnership?

 **CONNECTIONS**

Experienced co-teachers

- What are your prior experiences with establishing the co-teaching relationship?

Beginning co-teachers

- What is your comfort level with your current co-teacher?

Prospective co-teachers

- Are you excited about co-teaching? Nervous?
- If you, not an administrator, is initiating the co-teaching, how will you approach your administrator? How will you make your case that he or she should support co-teaching?

# II

# Practice Communication

# 4

# General Communication Advice

---

**CHAPTER CHECKLIST**

Once you have read this chapter, you should be able to

- ○ List three classroom or teaching principles that must be in place for you to be a successful co-teacher.
- ○ Describe three effective ways to communicate with your co-teacher.
- ○ Create a mutually agreed-on plan for how you will manage team disagreements.
- ○ Recognize the importance of both teachers adhering to the principles outlined in A Co-Teacher's Oath on page 52.

---

 *WHAT'S ON THE DVD?*

---

Sherry talks about how, as a general education teacher, she struggled with sharing control but learned to become comfortable in trusting her special education co-teacher, Craig. Sherry and Craig talk about the benefits of having a male and a female co-teacher in the classroom.

Tom, a special educator whose identity is protected in the DVD because he has not had good co-teaching experiences, talks about how he and his co-teacher found a way to teach together, regardless of their feelings about working together.

Ed and Tom talk about having difficult conversations with a co-teacher.

 **WHAT SHOULD I WATCH FOR ON THE DVD?**

- How did Sherry and Craig's co-teaching change as they gained trust in each other?

- How does having a common goal or philosophy with your co-teacher affect your classroom?

- What would be the best way for you to approach your co-teacher with a potential conflict? How can you present yourself in order to not appear confrontational?

- What is (or will be) hard for you to do, related to communicating with your co-teacher?

As previously noted, co-teaching has often been likened to a professional marriage (Friend & Cook, 2007). As a cursory survey of daytime television would reveal, there is a ubiquitous belief that good communication is the foundation for a successful marriage. Although this belief may be true, there is also abundant evidence that good communication is not easily achieved by marriage partners.

So, how can a co-teaching "marriage" establish good communication as a foundation and avoid any pitfalls related to communicating?

Each marriage is unique, and how the partners relate is idiosyncratic to their relationship. This is also true for co-teaching relationships. One pair of co-teachers may have a similar need for classroom organization, whereas another pair of co-teachers may have very different instructional styles. Both pairs can be very effective at co-teaching. What works for one team of co-teachers might not be effective for another; however, there are a few guiding practices that support successful co-teaching:

- Listening
- Respecting perspectives
- Communicating regularly
- Valuing differences
- Resolving disagreements

## LISTENING

One of the common clichés regarding communication in a relationship is the need to be good at listening. For better or worse, many clichés are often true; listening is a cornerstone of good communication. Listening is more than hearing the words that are being said; it requires being engaged and actively trying to understand the message that is being communicated (Friend & Cook, 2007).

One of the barriers to effective listening is our human tendency to want to offer advice or help to "fix" the situation. For example, consider a case in which two co-teachers had a lesson that was unsuccessful: The learners were not engaged, and both teachers often needed to redirect the students to help keep them on task. Following this lesson, the co-teachers discuss how to make the next lesson better. The special education teacher begins to vent her feelings of frustration with the off-task behaviors. The general education teacher quickly begins reassuring her teaching partner that most students in special education are often off task. The general education teacher then offers a "fix" to the problem: "We should take points away every time we have to remind them to complete the worksheet." The special education teacher is frustrated with this solution because, she admits, "I was having a bad day and needed you to listen to my feelings." Such miscommunication can create barriers between people. Parker Palmer eloquently stated that "we must remember a simple truth: the human soul does not want to be fixed, it wants simply to be seen and heard" (1998, p. 151).

To become an effective listener, try practicing. Often people have a tendency to interrupt the speaker or plan what they are going to say in response, or sometimes the mind wanders to tasks that must be accomplished. To practice listening, try to remain focused on the speaker and do not interrupt. You may also want to use phrases that will help to keep the conversation going, such as "help me understand" or "can you give me an example?" It is also important to be attentive to the talker. For example, nodding your head or making eye contact are ways to convey that you are interested in what is being discussed. It is not helpful to continually scan the room or to focus your attention on paperwork. Listening as a way of hearing what another person is trying to communicate can be very demanding of your attention. It also needs a quiet environment because of the need for focus (Palmer, 1998); therefore, you and your co-teacher may want to set aside time to discuss issues. During this time, try to minimize distractions (interruptions, talking on cell phones, checking e-mail).

## RESPECTING PERSPECTIVES

As previously discussed, general education teachers and special education teachers have different responsibilities, qualifications, and foundations for teaching that inform their perspectives. Beyond their different professional background, co-teachers may also have different teaching styles. Each of the co-teachers brings these perspectives, experiences, and concerns to the relationship. There may be items that can be negotiated between the teachers (classroom management, instructional strategies) and items that are nonnegotiable (cheating, disrespect). See Box 4.1 for a Teaching Beliefs

---

**BOX 4.1**    **Teaching Beliefs Questionnaire**

---

Both co-teachers should answer the following questions. Once both teachers have finished composing their answers, they should discuss their answers with each other. These questions are intended to facilitate a discussion of how the co-teaching relationship will work. Please note any areas that you may need to negotiate with each other.

1. What are your beliefs about the classroom environment?

    Noise (What is too loud?)

    Placement of desks (teacher and students)

    Layout of classroom (consider traffic flow, computers, group versus individual space)

    Bulletin boards (What will they have? Who is responsible?)

2. What are your beliefs about classroom management?

    Discipline

    Behavior plans (whole-class charts or individual charts)

    Reinforcers (tokens, praise, prizes, free time)

    Classroom rules

    Penalties for infractions of classroom rules

    Students eating or drinking in class

3. What are your teaching beliefs (preferences) for instruction?

    Small groups (pair and share, group projects)

    Individual (guided and individual practice)

    Lectures and labs

    Reading assignments

4. What are your beliefs about co-teaching?

5. What are your concerns about inclusion?

6. What are your concerns about co-teaching?

7. What do you think are potential benefits of co-teaching?

8. How can you express your personal teaching philosophy in a co-taught class?

   Once the questionnaire is completed, the co-teachers should share their responses. During this conversation, both co-teachers should explore areas they have in common and areas of possible disagreement.

*Source:* deBettencourt & Howard (2007).

---

Questionnaire that should assist co-teachers in identifying issues or concerns that may affect the ongoing relationship between the teachers.

    Respect for individual experience, perspective, and standards is a foundation for working with someone. Each teacher must demonstrate respect for the other or students in the classroom will sense the lack of respect. This can quickly escalate into classroom chaos, as students will attempt to divide the teachers whenever the opportunity presents itself. Such behavior can diminish the focus on instruction and force the two teachers to focus on classroom management. A classroom in chaos is a miserable situation for both teachers. This type of situation can be avoided by starting with a foundation of mutual respect, which can be enhanced through regular communication.

## COMMUNICATING REGULARLY

During the school day, co-teachers may have multiple interactions with each other. These interactions may be simple, such as identifying which teacher is going to make copies of the lab assignment, or more complicated, such as deciding which teacher is going to take the lead in calling a student's parent regarding disruptive classroom behavior. In addition to delivering instruction—the primary focus of any teacher's day—there may be parent conferences, committee meetings, and professional development activities that require teacher time and focus. These responsibilities may limit co-teachers' ability to arrange time for meetings to discuss more sensitive issues such as difficulties modifying instruction, feelings about the co-teaching relationship, concerns regarding classroom management, or related issues.

Despite the presence of multiple barriers, co-teachers must prioritize time for meeting with each other (Murawski, 2005). Joint planning time has been identified as a factor in the success of the co-teaching relationship (Howard & Potts, 2009). Co-teachers may need to be creative in finding co-planning time: They may need to ask for this time, meet after school at a coaching practice, meet online via instant messaging systems, or speak on the telephone after school. Some co-teachers have been known to carpool to school together—a great way to find co-planning time! The following issues should be considered as co-teachers plan for regular meeting time:

1. Formats for communicating

   Consider the realities of a teacher's day: Can there always be time for a face-to-face meeting? Or, can some information be conveyed through e-mail, a quick note, or an after-school telephone call? Both teachers need to discuss which formats might be best for them, as some people respond better to some forms of communication than others. Sometimes, a quick conversation in the hallway may be sufficient; for other information, a face-to-face planning meeting may be needed. Different formats will work for each team; the important consideration is that there must be communication.

2. Formal versus informal

   As previously discussed, informal, quick hallway conversations may be appropriate for communicating certain information. Other information (planning, accommodations, parental contact) may need to have a formal face-to-face meeting. Some teams have found that having a once-a-week scheduled meeting is a good way to ensure there is sufficient time to discuss co-teaching issues more thoroughly (this is an excellent use of co-planning time). Other teams have found that quick notes, e-mails, and hallway conversations can be used to discuss the day-to-day logistics of co-teaching. Other teams report that having a "debrief" telephone call at home once or twice per week allows them time to de-compress and connect with each other. Some teams connect with each other by spending time once or twice per month after school at the local coffee shop.

One of the advantages of a scheduled face-to-face meeting is that it provides structure to ensure that pairs address co-teaching consider-ations. Given the hectic pace of teaching, a regularly scheduled time (whether a formal meeting or coffee chat) provides the opportunity to address issues that may be ongoing or ones that have just arisen. An-other advantage to the formal meeting is that notes taken can be used to document various issues. This documentation might include accom-modations tried with a specific student, notes on curricular modifica-tions, and progress on IEP goals.

Although informal communication such as e-mail, hallway chats, or telephone updates are not always scheduled, they allow teachers to adjust to the immediacy of teaching. This can help a team make adjust-ments or reassignments, or ensure that both teachers are "in the loop."

Whether a team primarily uses a formal planning meeting or in-formal conversations, both team members should be comfortable with the format. In many situations, a combination of informal "chats" and formal planning time may be needed. Both teachers need to identify their preferences and compare their calendars.

3. Length and content

   The frequency and length of time for meetings should depend on what the teachers need to discuss or resolve. Again, a regularly scheduled time provides structure for the communication. It is probably not help-ful to schedule meetings for more than 2 hours on an occasional basis. People become tired when a meeting lasts too long, thus diminishing the meeting's usefulness. It is also not helpful to "save up" issues in hopes of resolving all issues in a marathon meeting. Such a delay may mean that the co-teachers must revisit an incident from several weeks in the past when there are more immediate concerns to address. Or, when issues are not quickly addressed, it can appear that one teacher is creating a grievance list, and the meeting can deteriorate into a gripe session. A frequently scheduled, regular meeting of moderate duration will be more productive for the team.

4. Appropriate number of interactions

   Often a new co-teaching team wants to have frequent meetings on a variety of topics. As the team becomes more established, fewer meet-ings may become the norm. Both team members need to feel that the meetings, chats, or e-mails are appropriate and beneficial to working together. There can be problems when one team member wants to have more frequent or longer meetings than the other. In this case, pairs need to compromise so that both team members are invested in maintaining communication.

5.  Respect for the time of each teacher

    Both team members must be willing to accept that each teacher has different responsibilities. The special education teacher must attend IEP meetings. The general education teacher must attend grade- or content-level meetings. These other commitments may reduce or limit the number and frequency of team meetings. This can cause frustration for either or both members of the team, as it will limit their ability to problem-solve issues that will arise within the team.

    Each team member must strive to respect and understand the responsibilities of the other team member (Murawski & Dieker, 2008). This is far easier to accomplish theoretically than in the day-to-day dynamic of the teaching relationship. Recognize that last-minute changes are going to happen, meetings will be cancelled, and often it may be difficult to communicate complex issues in a short time. Try to respect that each member of the team is "juggling" his or her responsibilities and understand that inevitably something may arise that will upend a scheduled meeting.

## VALUING DIFFERENCES

*Infinite diversity in infinite combinations*
(*Star Trek;* Aroeste & Senensky, 1968)

There is much diversity in the co-teaching universe. Consider that the teachers in a team may differ in gender, age, personality, culture, teacher education, and experience. Inevitably, all of these differences may contribute to difficulties in establishing rapport with each other, communicating effectively, and synchronizing teaching styles. Although the potential difficulties are vast, the importance of simply respecting each other cannot be overstated.

Although these differences may create difficulties in how the team functions, they also provide an opportunity to bring other perspectives, knowledge, and insight. Co-teachers can learn from each other and expand their own teaching experience and, by embracing the differences, become a stronger team. For example, consider a co-teaching team that has an experienced teacher paired with a less-experienced teacher. The experienced teacher brings knowledge of classroom routines, teaching, and working with parents. The inexperienced teacher brings enthusiasm for teaching, comfort using new technology, and updated content knowledge. Although there may be some "bumps" or issues needing resolution, the strengths each has can create an instructional balance that serves all of their students.

As teams work to establish their relationship, the issue of boundaries between professional and personal lives may become relevant. Some team teachers become friendly outside of work and enjoy spending time with each other. Other teams may function well as a team within the school but want to maintain some distance in their personal lives. Each team must negotiate these boundaries in a manner that works for both members. For example, are telephone calls after dinner welcome? Does one team member want to discuss his or her personal issues (divorce, children, and finances) with the other? Do the team members want to socialize outside of school?

Often individuals may have differing views on these issues, and the team will need to resolve this. One team member may feel that too much planning time is devoted to listening to the other teacher "vent" about his or her dating situation. Or, one team member may be uncomfortable spending too much weekend time with the other teacher. Personal boundaries need to be respected. Both team members must identify their individual comfort level with personal disclosures. For example, how will they make sure to respect each other's privacy and confidential conversations and recognize the other teacher's need for personal space? Trust is a vital component of any co-teaching relationship. Personal or family issues that are discussed should be kept between the two teachers. Each teacher must respect the privacy of the other. There should be no gossiping about your teaching partner in the teacher's lounge!

Another issue that can arise with some teams: When is a close relationship too close? For example, some teaching partners enjoy spending time with each other. They may have dinner out with their teaching partners and spouses, or they may choose to vacation with their spouses and their teaching partners. Other co-teaching teams may enjoy having a good work relationship but want to keep their work and personal lives separate. So, what if one co-teacher wants to spend time outside of school with his or her partner (and family) and the other co-teacher would like more personal space (and weekends free of the co-teacher)? Both teachers need to talk about their preferences, and they will need to come to an acceptable resolution for both teachers.

## RESOLVING DISAGREEMENTS

When a co-teaching team "clicks," the experience can be mutually supportive for both teachers (Austin, 2001). This can increase their job satisfaction and teaching effectiveness. However, when two people share the same classroom, occasional disagreements (e.g., preferred room temperature, preferred location of materials, responsibility for putting materials away) are inevitable. A disagreement does not have to escalate into a decision to end a teaching partnership; both teachers should strive to resolve the disagreement in a professional manner. If the disagreement goes unresolved, both team members can become unhappy. This can be a demoralizing situation for everyone, including the students.

Each member of the team should focus on respecting the other. Even when there is a disagreement, team members should focus on being polite in expressing their viewpoints. Some disagreements can be resolved by listening to the other perspective before commenting. Other disagreements can be diffused with a sincere apology. The Problem-Solving Worksheet (see Figure 4.1) offers a structured format for resolving concerns.

## Problem-Solving Worksheet

Team members:_____        Date/time:_____

Purpose of meeting:_____        Next meeting:_____

Student(s) (if applicable):_____

Agenda items:                          Discussion:

1.

2.

3.

Resolution/follow-up:        Responsible person:        Due date:

1.

2.

3.

How will progress be monitored?

**Figure 4.1.** Problem-Solving Worksheet. (DEBETTENCOURT, LAURIE U.; HOWARD, LORI, A., EFFECTIVE SPECIAL EDUCATION TEACHER: PRACTICAL GUIDE FOR SUCCESS, THE, 1st Edition, © 2007. p. 22. Reprinted by permission of Pearson Education, Inc., Upper Saddle River, NJ.)

Obviously, there is a continuum of disagreements. Some may be relatively minor, whereas others may be more fundamental to what each teacher believes is his or her role as a teacher. In some cases, one teacher may feel that the area of disagreement is very important, whereas the other teacher may feel that it is of minor significance and the other is "blowing something out of proportion." In these cases, it is vital to respectfully listen to the other person without diminishing his or her concerns or feelings. Both teachers in the partnership must feel that their concerns, opinions, and perspectives can be heard and valued by the other teacher.

Sometimes disagreements can be resolved by remembering that each teacher has specific knowledge and experience they bring to the partnership. For example, a special education teacher has specific training on IEPs and the importance of accommodations or modifications. The general education teacher has specific knowledge about the curriculum. A disagreement may occur due to the need to incorporate some modifications that reduce curriculum content. As each teacher listens to the other's perspective, a compromise that benefits the student and resolves the disagreement can be identified.

Another consideration for each team member is self-management. Disagreements can become emotional, causing tension between the two partners. This tension can provoke feelings of anger, bitterness, and frustration. These feelings may hinder the ability of the partners to address the actual disagreement: One teacher may wish to avoid conflict, so he or she withdraws from the situation; the other may be more confrontational. For example, one teacher may be uncomfortable with students gathering at the door to wait for the bell to ring, whereas the other teacher has no problem with it. When the uncomfortable teacher brings this issue up, the other teacher may rapidly agree to stop the practice. However, in future meetings, the more passive teacher, wanting to keep the peace, does not contribute issues or concerns. Over the course of the school year, less and less is accomplished in planning meetings. During classroom instruction, the teachers engage in less teaming and more turn-taking.

Another teacher may want to assert a position, so he or she attempts to persuade the other of the correctness of the position. For example, the two teachers are discussing how a unit test is being created and how it will be given. There is a disagreement about grading the section of the test that requires several long essay answers. One teacher expresses concern over several students who are not good writers. The other teacher insists that the longer essays are the only way to adequately assess student knowledge of the content. The teacher who insists that the essays are needed notes that writing is an essential skill and students must be able to write. The conversation continues with one teacher verbally insisting on the writing and how important it is to content knowledge. This may result in the partner feeling bullied into accepting a situation. Sometimes, despite good intentions, physical reactions to anger and stress can cause a situation to escalate.

---

**BOX** **4.2** **Fight-or-flight response and self-management strategies**

The *fight-or-flight response* happens when the brain senses something as a threat. It also happens during a disagreement or a conflict leading to anger. Many people experience knots in the stomach or clenching of the jaw. These are signals that the body senses a threat and is preparing to fight or flee from the situation. The body activates the sympathetic nervous system, which also inhibits the parasympathetic nervous system. Basically, heart rate, blood pressure, and breathing increase due to the release of epinephrine and norepinephrine (Kosslyn & Rosenberg, 2005). This causes more oxygen to flow to the muscles to prepare the person to either fight or flee. Once this process has started, it is very difficult to return to a calm state. This response also makes it very difficult to focus on a conversation or provide alternative solutions to a disagreement.

One of the best (and easiest) ways to help counteract this physiological reaction is to change your breathing. Because the physiological response is to increase the rate of breathing, it helps to slow your breathing down, hence the common advice to take a deep breath when confronted with a difficult situation. You may have also been told to count to 10 when angry.

Stress can amplify this reaction, so helping to manage your own stress can help your problem solving. The following are some common sense reminders to help you self-manage:

- Eat a healthy breakfast and lunch.
- Exercise regularly; consider taking a yoga class—it will help with the breathing.
- Take at least 2 hours of relaxation weekly.
- Write down your thoughts and concerns in a reflection journal.
- Maintain a sense of perspective.
- Seek support from friends.
- Watch a funny movie—laughing is a great stress reducer.

---

See Box 4.2 for a discussion of the fight-or-flight response and strategies to help manage responses to conflict.

## SEEKING OTHER ASSISTANCE

On occasion, a disagreement or ongoing disagreements may require another person to help resolve the situation. The team may need to seek the help of the principal, assistant principal, special education department chair, or other administrator. The administrator can act as a neutral party so that both team members feel their concerns will be heard and addressed (Friend & Cook, 2007). The administrator will help to mediate the concerns of the team members.

When seeking help from an administrator, both team members should provide a dispassionate statement of the situation and be receptive to possible solutions. It may also be helpful to provide a summary of previous attempts to resolve the situation. Ultimately, the best resolution is one that will work for both teachers and their students. See Box 4.3 for a discussion of conflict resolution strategies.

The team may also request additional professional development time on issues related to co-teaching. This might include observations of successful teams within the same school, observations of teams at other schools that teach similar grades or content, attending a workshop or conference

---

**BOX 4.3 Conflict resolution strategies**

There are semester-long courses and entire sections in bookstores devoted to resolving conflicts. Most teachers can benefit from some training or education in resolving conflicts, whether with other teachers, administrators, or parents. Given the complexity and breadth of the subject, it is difficult to fully address the concepts within the confines of this text; however, teachers should be familiar with the concepts of *compromise* and *negotiation*.

*Compromise* is the idea that an individual (teacher) gives up something and, in return, the other individual (teacher) also gives up something (Friend & Cook, 2007). This solution can be useful when there is a time constraint and an agreement is needed quickly. It can also be a little like *Let's Make a Deal*. It provides a way for both teachers to invest in the outcome.

For example, one teacher may need to attend an after-school meeting while the team is creating a unit plan. The compromise might be that the teacher with the meeting will grade the student homework for the week while the other teacher develops the unit plan. Each teacher gets something (less grading, time for the meeting) desirable.

*Negotiation* is the idea that two individuals agree on a solution to a problem or disagreement through discussion (Friend & Cook, 2007). This can be useful in resolving conflict as it encourages a "give and take" between the individuals. Generally, a successful negotiation focuses on the issues, prioritizes those issues with the greatest likelihood of agreement, and attempts to remove emotionally laden language from the discussion (Friend & Cook, 2007). See Ury (1991) for a complete discussion of negotiation.

Consider a conflict between co-teachers over modifying an experimental lab for their classroom. One teacher wants the lab to be conducted as it always has been; the other teacher sees a need to simplify some of the directions and provide more explicit guidance on how the experiment is to be conducted. This could be a very difficult situation, as often teaching beliefs about content are involved; however, the two teachers decide to sit down together and review the lab experiment. During this conversation, each teacher contributes to the outcome. The teacher who wanted to do it the "same old way" is able to define significant portions of the lab that must be conducted. The other teacher writes up a new lab assignment with a graphic organizer that will be used by all of the students.

on co-teaching, or asking for in-class support through a co-teaching specialist visiting the classroom. Often, teams can benefit from seeing or discussing with other team teachers how disagreements can be resolved. Some teams may benefit from professional mediation to help strengthen the partnership and address areas of disagreement. Some school districts provide mediation assistance to co-teachers, and the team can request this.

Finally, there are some disagreements that cannot be resolved, and in such a case the team should consider ending the partnership. (See Chapter 13 for a discussion of how to dissolve a co-teaching team.) As co-teaching has been likened to a marriage, this decision can be analogous to seeking a "divorce." In divorce, the couple is often counseled to carefully consider the implications; it is similar when ending a co-teaching partnership. Again, an administrator will need to be involved, as pairings of co-teachers are often an administrative responsibility. See Chapter 13 for a more thorough discussion of administrator responsibilities and co-teaching, including when a team may need to be dissolved.

## CONCLUSION

After reading this chapter, the importance of mutual communication and respect should be apparent. Each team of co-teachers will develop its own style of working together and create a teaching dynamic that is unique to the partnership. Listening and respecting multiple opinions, varied educational and teaching experiences, and different ways of approaching instruction are important to building a successful co-teaching relationship.

When reviewing the chapter checklist, can you check the items as complete? Have you identified three principles that must be in place for co-teaching to work in your classroom? Have you and your co-teacher discussed three ways in which you will regularly communicate? Have you developed a plan for managing the inevitable disagreements that may arise with your co-teacher?

Co-teaching has been described as a teaching marriage (Friend & Cook, 2007). This analogy provides a framework for co-teachers to establish their classroom partnership. It may be helpful for both co-teachers to review A Co-Teacher's Oath, found on page 52 and on the accopanying DVD, as they begin or renew their partnership. This oath provides a forum for understanding the work and commitment it will take to make a productive co-teaching marriage work in a classroom.

 *REFLECTIONS*

- What are your preferences for communication (format, formal versus informal, and so on)?
- What are you prior experiences with resolving conflict?

# A Co-Teacher's Oath

As a responsible and caring member of this co-teaching team, I promise to do the following:

- Respect the perspectives of my co-teacher. Just because that isn't the way I would do it doesn't make it wrong.

- Put students and instruction at the center of my co-teaching relationship; it is because of the students that our team exists.

- Engage in best practices, recognizing that the goal of co-teaching is student success.

- Communicate with my co-teacher about classroom concerns.

- Support my co-teacher's decisions in front of the students. I recognize the importance of presenting a unified front.

- Take time to plan with my co-teacher on a regular basis.

- Celebrate our successes, whether they are with individual students or classwide.

- Evaluate and improve practices with my co-teacher to make our partnership stronger.

- Recognize that disagreements are inevitable and commit to working through difficult situations in a professional manner.


Signature: _____     Signature: _____


Role: _____     Role: _____

 **CONNECTIONS**

All co-teachers

• Think about your perspective and what shades the way you see the classroom. Consider the perspective of your co-teacher. Think about your teacher training, your professional development, your personality, your teaching style, and your level of comfort with asserting your needs. Consider the training, professional development, personality, teaching style, and assertiveness of your co-teacher. Are there similarities? What are the differences?

# 5

# The Ideal versus the Reality

---

## CHAPTER CHECKLIST

Once you have read this chapter, you should be able to

○ Recognize how your real-life co-teaching situation varies from your ideal.

○ Describe how each of your co-teaching situations varies and how you can adapt.

○ Create a plan with each of your co-teachers to manage your time and responsibilities.

○ Identify three items needed from your administrator to support your co-teaching.

---

 **WHAT'S ON THE DVD?**

---

Sherry talks about the support she and her co-teacher have received from administration to help them continue to teach together for several years.

Debbie, an administrator, talks about what good co-teaching looks like in the classroom and how co-teachers can improve their relationship.

Craig talks about the reality of co-teaching with multiple general education teachers.

**WHAT SHOULD I WATCH FOR ON THE DVD?**

- How can administrators help co-teachers work through the realities of co-teaching?
- How does Craig organize working with more than one co-teacher?

In previous chapters, we discussed foundations of co-teaching, including models, perspectives, communication, and conflict resolution. In each of these discussions was an implicit assumption that co-teaching involves two teachers—one special education and one general education. Ideally, two teachers would teach together for most of the school day and over a number of years. If they are elementary school teachers, for example, they may be assigned to teach a fourth-grade inclusive class together. If they are teaching middle or high school, they may be assigned to co-teach the same sections of a single discipline. They may teach together three periods of 9th grade language arts and one period of 11th grade language arts. Through the time spent preparing and teaching the same content with each other, they grow together as a team.

This ideal situation of co-teaching is rarely the norm. Often, an individual special education teacher will be assigned to co-teach with multiple general education teachers. For example, a special education teacher may be assigned to co-teach two sections of biology and an additional section of world history. In this situation, the special education teacher may have two separate co-teaching partners: one for the science classes and one for the history class.

The special education teacher must manage different curriculum goals and content for each of these classes but also the relationship with the two (or more) different general education teachers (Friend & Cook, 2007). Consider all of the factors that go into working with a teaching partner and the amount of time it takes to establish the relationship. This can overwhelm a special education teacher when he or she has more than one partner. Simply trying to remember each partner's pet peeves, instructional style, and planning preferences can be challenging.

## FINDING TIME

One of the barriers to successful co-teaching is the lack of time for planning and establishing rapport (deBettencourt & Howard, 2007). Often co-teachers find out that they have been assigned to teach together in the weeks before or in the beginning of the school year. There may be little time to meet together and acquaint themselves with each other. The time that is allocated for meeting may be spent on practical matters such as planning for instruction and identifying which students will need accommodations or modifications and how the classroom will be set up. Although these practical matters are vitally important, planning for them does not leave adequate time for teachers to discuss their teaching beliefs and preferred models of co-teaching and to preplan for difficulties (Linz, Heater, & Howard, 2008).

Once the school year begins, it can be even more difficult to find time to meet with multiple co-teaching partners. However, it is critical to the success of each co-teaching pair that partners find time to meet. Co-planning time with co-teachers is essential to success (Scruggs et al., 2007) and should be identified for all partnerships. Once the schedule of classes and planning time has been arranged, co-teachers should use their calendars or planners to identify times they can be available to meet with each other. Teachers may use computer software programs for time management of multiple tasks or projects to set up a potential meeting schedule at the start of the year. When there are multiple partners, it may be most helpful to have a regularly scheduled meeting on the planner.

Each partnership should identify items that require immediate attention, items that can be held until the next meeting, and when it may be appropriate to contact the other partner at home. For example, a telephone call from a complaining parent might warrant a quick chat before one partner communicates with the parent. A general concern about scores on a test might be addressed at the regularly scheduled weekly meeting. Each co-teaching pair will have to address these details; however, for an individual special education teacher this may require more written notes to ensure that each partner's preferences are respected. See Box 5.1 for suggestions about using technology to help manage this communication.

## MAINTAINING RELATIONSHIPS

Previous chapters discussed the importance of building the co-teaching relationship through trust, respect, and communication. These foundational skills are also necessary when co-teaching with multiple partners; however, there is the added dimension of maintaining separate relationships with each partner. Each co-teaching pair will make unique decisions about its relationship and teaching styles that should promote that team's success. Naturally, there may be a tendency to compare different teaching partners. This should be avoided! No teacher (or person) wants to feel that he or she is being compared to another teacher (or person) while striving to build a relationship.

Sometimes a co-teaching pair will gel and the partnership will be seamless and feel supportive (Austin, 2001); however, in other cases, a co-teaching pair may struggle to develop a working relationship. This can be particularly difficult when a special education teacher is a member of both of these co-teaching pairs simultaneously. The special education teacher must maintain a professional relationship with both general education teachers. On some days, it may feel as though the special education teacher

---

**BOX** $5.1$ | **Thinking outside the planning box**

---

Although face-to-face planning meetings are essential to building a good co-teaching partnership, they are not always possible. Consider how you and your co-teacher(s) can use technology or create communication strategies that work for you. Here are a few ideas:

1.  E-mail notes for updates (note that many school districts have confidentiality policies when using e-mail to communicate about specific students, so review your school's policy).

2.  File sharing for instructional planning: Files can be placed on a server so that both teachers can access and work with documents when they have time. There are also functions within many word processing programs that enable changes to be easily identified by both teachers (e.g., Microsoft Word's track changes feature).

3.  Teleconferencing for quick meetings when teachers are at different locations: Some programs (e.g., Skype) allow teachers to communicate via webcam through a computer. This might be useful to communicate when one or both teachers is out of the school building. Some teleconferencing programs also allow the sharing of documents so that both teachers could provide input.

4.  Text messaging through cell phones to communicate small amounts of information: This can provide a quick update or "heads up" about an upcoming concern.

5.  Other technology can also be used, depending on the team's preferences. For example, some cable television providers have a feature where Facebook and Twitter can be seen on the television screen. Teachers could read "tweets" while getting the local traffic and weather update on their television before leaving for school.

Note that teachers should be mindful of the need to be careful with privacy settings when using these technologies, as confidentiality of student information must be maintained.

---

is whiplashed between the joy of teaching and the despair of being in a dysfunctional partnership. Such a situation can be very emotionally and physically exhausting. There will be the temptation to vent to the general education teacher in the positive relationship about the other general education teacher. Again, this is to be avoided. Although it is difficult not to discuss the co-teaching relationship when it is painful, lacking in respect, and tiring, teachers need to avoid this as it violates the trust needed to work through the difficulties. The special education teacher is advised to seek a trustworthy person outside of the co-teaching relationships with whom to express these feelings—perhaps even someone outside of the school.

Each co-teaching relationship must be nurtured, and each is unique. The special education teacher who has multiple teaching partners must strive to foster a positive relationship with each of the other partners. This can be very time consuming and will require a conscious effort by the special education teacher. A supportive relationship with a general education teacher who appreciates the complexities of the different relationships is vital to helping ease the inevitable tensions.

## JUGGLING RELATIONSHIPS AND RESPONSIBILITIES

The previous discussion focused on the juggling that a special education teacher must manage with multiple teaching partners, but the support and understanding of the general education teacher in the partnership cannot be overstated. In most cases, both teachers are juggling myriad responsibilities that must be addressed as part of their teaching day (Friend & Cook, 2007). The general education teacher is often a member of a grade- or content-level team that addresses issues of curriculum, standardized testing, and content knowledge. The special education teacher is a member of IEP teams and may case-manage multiple students in special education. Both of these teachers must use effective time management. All partners in a co-teaching relationship need to appreciate the perspective of the other (Howard & Potts, 2009).

Respecting and valuing the responsibilities of each teacher in the partnership is much easier said than done. What happens when a test or quiz is not modified because the special education teacher was in an IEP meeting? What happens when there is an unexpected team meeting on test scores that the general education teacher must attend during planning time? All teachers in a co-teaching relationship should preplan for these situations as much as possible, but more important, remain flexible and open to problem-solving when they arise. Simply, you cannot preplan for all contingencies. However, a positive, flexible attitude can help to alleviate the tensions caused by such situations.

Sometimes it is impossible to juggle it all, and teachers should be able to discuss their priorities. What *must* we accomplish versus what do I *hope* to accomplish? Ideally, this discussion should take place regularly during joint planning time; however, the reality of teaching is that there may not be time to have a detailed discussion. It may be easiest to provide a quick verbal update and a one-page list of tasks or meetings that one teacher can share with the other teacher. This type of quick communication can help to foster trust between the teachers as they both juggle the demands on their time.

## ADMINISTRATOR SUPPORT

As co-teachers struggle to meet all of their responsibilities, they are often advised to seek administrative support; however, among the concerns affecting school districts' ability to support special education are overwhelming paperwork, inadequate district and administrative support, and the need for better-trained special and general education teachers (Council for Exceptional Children, 2001; Scruggs et al., 2007). Concurrent with these concerns are efforts to ameliorate the lack of support by providing more preparation for principals in the area of special education, co-teaching, and collaboration (Garrison-Wade, Sobel, & Fulmer, 2007).

Principals are encouraged to understand the special education laws (e.g., IDEA 2004) and vocabulary. They are also required to understand their responsibilities related to special education, such as participation at IEP meetings, ensuring that personnel are granted the time to meet their responsibilities, helping to ensure that least restrictive environments are maintained for all special education students, and committing to ensuring that the appropriate resources are available for meeting the needs of students with special needs (Green, 2008). These responsibilities are in addition to their role as school leader. It should be apparent that principals and administrators are also juggling multiple responsibilities and may have limited time to actively facilitate co-teaching partnerships.

So, although administrator support is acknowledged as an important factor in co-teaching success, what do co-teachers need from their administrators to be successful? As previously stated, co-planning time is essential, and the administrator's master schedule should accommodate such time for all co-teaching pairs. There has been much discussion and emphasis on co-planning time; however, there are other ways for administrators to support co-teaching and collaboration. According to Hines (2008), these include the following:

1. Provide opportunities to share positive co-teaching experiences at faculty meetings.
2. Ask co-teaching pairs to document their teaming activities.
3. Communicate with other principals regarding co-teaching and inclusion.
4. Encourage co-teaching pairs to visit classrooms of successful co-teaching teams at other schools.
5. Assist co-teaching pairs to develop goals for the team.
6. Provide professional development opportunities in co-teaching.
7. Observe co-teaching classrooms and provide feedback to the teachers.
8. Help to mediate and resolve conflicts that a co-teaching pair may have.

## TEACHER EVALUATION

One of the responsibilities of administrators and principals is to manage personnel, including evaluating teachers. As a new co-teaching team is working to establish its relationship, there may be concerns about how the *team* will be evaluated, as well as each individual teacher of the team (Patterson & Protheroe, 2000). This can also be a concern when an experienced teacher is paired with a newly hired teacher who will be evaluated more often during the probationary period.

Because the principal or administrator must evaluate the effectiveness of the teaching, this can become a barrier for co-teaching teams in soliciting

---

BOX **5.2** **Administrator checklist for supporting co-teaching**

---

Do you provide or do the following?

- Recognize positive co-teaching experiences schoolwide
- Congratulate co-teaching pairs on their achievements, whether related to student academic achievement or to problem-solving a difficult situation
- Ensure that every co-teaching pair has co-planning time
- Support professional development for your co-teaching teams
- Send co-teachers together to conferences or workshops
- Provide release time so that co-teaching pairs can visit successful co-teaching teams at other schools
- Regularly observe co-taught classrooms
- Invest the time needed to develop a co-teaching pair
- Keep effective co-teaching pairs together for multiple years
- Help co-teaching pairs resolve their differences
- Seek out professional development opportunities for yourself in the areas of special education, inclusion, and co-teaching
- Welcome suggestions from your co-teaching teams on how to better support their needs

---

support from the administrator. Individuals within a co-teaching pair that is struggling may be reluctant to honestly address these issues with an administrator for fear of receiving a negative performance review. However, principals often must engage in classroom observation before completing a review. It is difficult to "mask" or hide a struggling co-teaching situation when the actual teaching is being observed. All co-teachers need to remember that feedback can help them improve their relationship.

Principals and administrators are reminded that effective co-teaching needs time to develop, support through professional development, and an appreciation of the efforts of the team. As previously discussed, as more schools move toward inclusion and co-teaching models, principals need to increase their knowledge of how best to support these co-teaching teams. See Box 5.2 for ideas for administrators to help support co-teaching.

Principals should also acknowledge that how co-teaching looks and feels in a classroom will vary from team to team. When observing a co-teaching pair, it is important to recognize that the instruction to all students should be effective and that different models of co-teaching may be used. Therefore, the principal (or administrator) should identify whether the co-teachers are using effective instructional strategies for inclusion (discussed further in Chapter 13). The principal should also recognize how the teachers manage the classroom, provide the instruction, and work together to accomplish these tasks. Box 5.3 provides suggestions to co-teachers for preparing for classroom observations.

---

**BOX** **5.3** | **Preparing for co-teaching classroom observation**

- Have a preobservation conference with your administrator, if possible. Discuss with the administrator your joint philosophy of co-teaching and what he or she should expect to see during the observation.
- If co-teaching is new to your administrator, consider providing him or her with a resource about co-teaching that is specifically aimed at administrators. McDuffie's (2010) *The Co-Teaching Guide for Special Education Administrators: From Guesswork to What Really Works* may be a good choice.
- Provide your administrator with a copy of your lesson plan. Even if you do not always write out a full and complete plan, create one for your observation that includes components discussed in Chapter 10.
- Plan for the postobservation conference by engaging in some postlesson reflection with your co-teacher. Be ready to tell your administrator what went well, what did not work as planned, and what you might change in the future.

---

## SOLICITING ADMINISTRATOR SUPPORT

Often, co-teaching pairs are assigned by the administrator or principal; however, sometimes two teachers may be so excited about the possibilities of co-teaching together that they ask for the opportunity. They need to elicit the support of the school administration for this endeavor. It may be helpful to encourage the administrator (or principal) by providing information as to why these two teachers believe they will be effective co-teachers. What can each partner bring to this co-teaching relationship that will benefit all of the students in the class? Why is this a good co-teaching pairing?

In other cases, a successful co-teaching team may want to continue co-teaching in the next year (Linz et al., 2008). The co-teachers may want to ask the administrator to come to their classroom for an observation of their effective partnership or provide an e-mail update regarding a very successful lesson that they taught. The team should consider how to "market" or sell the administrator on the effectiveness of the pairing. Has student achievement increased? Are IEP goals being met? The team should collect this data throughout the school year and be able to provide the data to the administrator as support of the team's effectiveness.

## CONCLUSION

While reading through this chapter, you should have noted the importance of establishing unique relationships among multiple co-teaching pairs. Often, an individual special education teacher may have multiple co-teaching partners. Managing these different teaching relationships is challenging and time consuming. Co-teachers are often advised to solicit administrator support to help them manage all of their responsibilities. Administrators' understanding of the issues related to special education, collaboration, and co-teaching is vital to successful inclusion programs.

Please review the chapter checklist. Can you describe how your individual co-teaching situation varies from the ideal? Have you created a plan with your co-teacher to effectively plan and communicate? Can you identify three items that you need from your administrator to support your co-teaching?

In Chapter 4, co-teaching was compared to a marriage. The current chapter focused on the realities of establishing a working relationship when multiple teaching partners are involved. The foundations of good communication, trust, respect, and flexibility are still important when there are multiple co-teaching partners. Each relationship must be nurtured and is unique.

 ## REFLECTIONS

- What are your concerns heading into a co-teaching partnership?
- What bumps in the road have you experienced in the past when working with others?

 ## CONNECTIONS

All co-teachers

- How will you solve the issues that arise because of the difference between the ideal co-teaching situation and the realities of co-teaching situations?
- How will it work if you and/or one of your co-teachers works with more than one teacher? What will you do to ensure success for the different partnerships?

# 6

# Co-Teachers
## Beginning the Conversation

---

**CHAPTER CHECKLIST**

Once you have read this chapter, you should be able to

○ List important items for you and your co-teacher to talk about in initial conversations.

○ Be comfortable starting the initial conversation with your co-teacher.

---

*Note:* There are no DVD video clips for Chapter 6.

### THE PRECONVERSATION: GETTING TO KNOW ALL ABOUT YOU

Co-teachers spend a great deal of time together. Even if they co-teach just 50 minutes a day, that is over 125 hours in a school year, not including planning time and conference time and problem-solving time. Two professionals who work together that closely need to start their relationship by getting to know each other. It is a good idea to meet for coffee, preferably away from school, and engage in casual conversation about life. Now is a good time to swap backgrounds, recognizing that there are pieces of our personal lives that are pertinent to our teaching. For instance, if one of the co-teachers is going through a major life change such as marriage or divorce, the other co-teacher can be more understanding

---

**BOX** | **6.1** | **Getting-to-know-you conversation starters**

- How did you come to be a teacher? What drew you to this grade or discipline?
- What do you think is most important for me to know about you?
- What are your interests outside of teaching? What do you do in your spare time?
- How long have you been at this school?
- Are we comfortable calling each other at home?

---

of mood changes or distractibility if he or she knows about the situation. Remember, though, that not all co-teachers are comfortable with having a close personal relationship; take time to set up personal boundaries, as discussed in Chapter 4. Also take some time, before delving into the practical logistics of teaching together, to build trust. We are not recommending that you do "trust fall" exercises, just that you take time to get to know one another enough to feel comfortable in expressing your opinions and concerns with one another. See Box 6.1 for ideas on getting the conversation started.

## THE CONVERSATION

There is little as vitally important to the success of a co-teaching partnership as what happens in the initial conversations about the coming year. Even if they know each other from teaching in the same school, co-teachers are going to have to get to know each other in a new way, and the first meetings set the tone for the relationship. In addition to keeping in mind the good communication strategies detailed in Chapter 4—specifically, respecting your co-teacher and his or her perspective—it is important to begin to agree on the details of what your classroom will look like, feel like, and be.

Prior to the first planning meeting, both teachers should do some homework. If the content is new to the special education teacher, he or she should look into the state or national standards and at least be familiar with the general concepts that are covered in that grade level. Even if the special education teacher is not a content expert, he or she needs to understand and study the curriculum enough to be engaged in the planning process (Kloo & Zigmond, 2008). In return, the general education teacher will want to bring materials and ideas that he or she has used to teach this content in the past. If the general education teacher has been teaching for a number of years, the team may find it most efficient to take existing materials and adapt them. In addition, if he or she has access, the general education teacher will want to review relevant parts of student IEPs before the first planning meeting so that both teachers' background knowledge of the students is the same.

It is logical to begin the discussion with the topics that are most persistent throughout the school year and all of the co-teaching responsibilities. Get to know each other's preferences for how to communicate and pass information, keeping in mind that not everyone is equally comfortable with all modes of communication. Along with deciding on *how* co-teachers will communicate, it is important to set shared expectations for *why* and *to what end* co-teachers will communicate. See Box 6.2 for questions co-teachers should discuss related to boundaries for what and how to communicate.

In addition, in those first meetings, co-teachers need to decide on the logistics of their shared classroom. What will the flow of the class period look like? What models of co-teaching are co-teachers presently comfortable with, and will they need to work on expanding to use more models? How will they decide on and establish routines and rules in the classroom? How will the co-teachers present themselves to the students as a co-teaching pair? See Chapter 9 for a more detailed discussion of these issues.

Noting the universal understanding that co-planning time is essential to successful co-teaching (Friend & Cook, 2007; Magiera, Smith, Zigmond, & Gerbaner, 2005; Mastropieri et al., 2005; Scruggs, Mastropieri, & McDuffie, 2007), early discussions between co-teachers should have a heavy emphasis on how they will juggle planning for the co-taught class. These discussions need to include agreeing on when co-teachers will dedicate time to plan together, made easier if administrators have assigned them co-planning time during the school day; how far in advance they will plan; and what roles they will each take in the planning process. In situations where the special education teacher is not a content expert, it is likely that the general education teacher will bring the content knowledge to the planning table, whereas the special education teacher will focus on adjusting curriculum to meet the needs of all students and improving content

---

**BOX 6.2  Questions for discussion: communication**

- What will our regular schedule for detailed planning or discussions be?
- How is it best to get last-minute information to each other?
- Can we communicate via e-mail? Telephone calls at home?
- How will we interact with parents? As a team? Separately? As requests come in?
- How will we deal with and communicate issues such as students who are not performing well or who need extra help?
- How will we avoid students asking one of us a question, then going to the other if they do not like the first answer?
- On what kinds of decisions should we always consult each other?
- What kinds of things should we each handle independently?

See Chapter 4 for additional information.

# Co-Teaching Planning Checklist

## STANDARDS

Did we . . .

- Use the standards as the focal point of the lesson
- Include opportunities to connect to IEP goals

## ASSESSMENT

Did we . . .

- Start with the end in mind
- Include formative assessment
- Include summative assessment
- Assess in a variety of formats
  - Paper-and-pencil
  - Project-based
  - Oral
  - Presentations
- Agree on grading procedures
  - Who is responsible
  - Differentiating grading based on student needs
  - Use of rubrics
- Talk about homework
  - How much to assign
  - How often to assign
  - How to grade
  - Accepting late work
  - Procedures for turning in homework

## ACCOMMODATIONS/MODIFICATIONS

Did we . . .

- Address any non–content-related IEP goals
- Address appropriate content-related IEP goals
- Consider needs of individual students for assignments and classwork
- Discuss how to provide accommodations/modifications without alienating students with disabilities

## INSTRUCTIONAL STRATEGIES

Did we consider including . . .

- Mnemonics
- Graphic organizers
- Cooperative learning strategies
- Progress monitoring
- Peer-assisted learning strategies

## LOGISTICS

Who will prepare . . .

- Materials
- Tests

Did we plan for . . .

- Seating
- Roles in instruction
- Roles in discipline
- Classroom movement patterns

*Key:* IEP, individualized education program.

knowledge to increase his or her effectiveness. In the case where both teachers are content experts, they may decide that they will take turns taking the content lead in planning.

A good tool to use when discussing specific lessons is the Co-Teaching Planning Checklist found on page 68 and also on the accompanying DVD. The checklist reminds co-teachers to think about good instructional and planning practices, such as including multiple types of assessment, and also to link special education needs and practices to the general education classroom. For instance, one of the items on the checklist is "include opportunities to connect to IEP goals." Though the special educator should naturally have this on his or her radar, using the checklist provides the co-teachers the opportunity to discuss and think about the connection together and to systematically connect IEP goals to classroom activities. For example, co-teachers can create cooperative learning activities designed to allow a student with a disability to work on IEP goals related to working with peers.

Finally, before the students ever walk in the door, the co-teachers must talk about classroom policy. If the two teachers have divergent policies on behavior management or classroom routines, it is important that they come to a consistent understanding of what the policies will be in their shared classroom. Inconsistency will lead to the students playing "mom and dad games" with the co-teachers, going to one teacher for permission or absolution when they do not get what they want from the other teacher. See Box 6.3 for examples of questions co-teachers should talk about related to classroom management. See Chapter 9 for additional information on classroom management.

Figure 6.1 reflects minutes taken at an initial meeting between two people co-teaching with each other for the first time. Note that these co-teachers talked about what they were going to do to be seen as a team, as well as forming a plan for how to begin instruction and evaluate their teaching. These team members also talked about important issues such as grading, classroom and attendance policies, how they will plan, and how they will work with parents.

---

**BOX 6.3 Questions for discussion: classroom management**

- What will our policies be for gum, food, and drink in class?
- What will students be expected to have in front of them (e.g., pencil sharpened, paper out, book out, warm-up activity complete) when the bell rings?
- How will we communicate our policies to the students?
- What will consequences be for inappropriate behavior?
- How will we project that we are both classroom leaders?

See Chapter 9 for additional information.

Items discussed August 25 (before start of school)

*Approach to instruction*

Seen as a team
- Let's put both names on door and bulletin boards
- All materials will have both our names

Models of co-teaching
- What are we most comfortable with?
- Let's try One Teach, One Observe/Assist, Station Teaching, and Team Teaching.
- We can get to know each other with the One Teach, One Assist model. Then, Station Teaching allows us to work with smaller groups of kids. Once we are comfortable with each other and content instruction, let's try to really team teach.

Build in time to check/evaluate to see if team is working
- Let's plan to check in every couple of weeks to make sure that we are okay with what is happening in the classroom and for the students.

*Standards/grading policies*

Achievement and standardized testing
- All of our students are going to have to take the end of the year standardized tests. They all need to pass to get their diplomas. We need to make sure that all of the students can learn the material. We better plan to include test preparation in our warm ups. Our unit tests should also have standardized type test questions.

Grading
- We need to make sure that all accommodations/modifications are made in the instruction. We need to figure out how to address late and incomplete homework, class participation, and a rubric for their projects. Maybe we should use a point system that rewards all students for completing and turning in homework. The project/presentation rubric needs to be differentiated for students with individualized education programs (IEPs) to allow for extra time, shorter writing components, and other issues.

*Classroom policies*
- We need to make sure that all students know our expectations for classroom behavior.
- Hands should be raised, and students should be called on before speaking. During individual work time it is okay to go to the pencil sharpener, but not okay to chat with neighbors. Students need to speak respectfully and courteously to everyone in the class.
- Politeness should be emphasized. All students are to be polite in class.

*Curriculum/program of studies*

Instructional routines
- We will need to establish the following and let's take turns doing each of these so that students realize we are both teaching the class.
  *Attendance*
  *Warm ups*—These can also include test taking strategies and sample test questions.
  *Homework collection*—Let's do this after we have gone over it with the class.
  *Exit routine*—Let's have students write in their planners, put things away, and then line up to leave before the bell rings.

Unit/lesson planning
- We need to use our regular co-planning time to make sure that our instruction is focused on the program of studies for our content. The general education teacher will take the lead on content, while the special education teacher will take the lead with strategies, materials, and extra resources. We'll also need to address the following on a regular basis:

**Figure 6.1.** Co-planning meeting minutes. (From Howard, L., &. Potts, E.A. [2009]. Using co-planning time: Strategies for a successful co-teaching marriage. *TEACHING Exceptional Children Plus, 5*[4], Article 2. Reproduced with permission, copyright © 2009 by the Council for Exceptional Children, Inc. www.cec.sped.org. All rights reserved.)

*Modifications of the curriculum*—When will we need to extensively cover specific content? What content could be enrichment versus what they really need to know? What can we modify and still prepare our students for the standardized test?

*Preparation of materials*—We should share this responsibility.

*Who teaches what content?*—The general education teacher will be responsible for teaching the content (when using the One Teach, One Assist model) but we both need to teach content when using the Station Teaching and Team Teaching models. Let's plan for the special ed teacher to do the warm up and test preparation to start the semester. Later, let's discuss how we can both teach together.

*Parents*

Back-to-School Night
- We both need to be there, and we should let parents know that we are both teaching the class.

Parent conferences
- We both should plan to be there, and parents should know that we are a team.

Parent communication
- We will both do and keep each other in the "loop."
- Parents should know that they can contact either one of us, but we will communicate the issue to the other teacher.

*Note:* We also need to make sure that this works for us. Maybe we should just have lunch together once a week so that we can decompress and chat. There is so much to plan for that it is overwhelming. We need to support and help each other. After all, we are in this together!

## AFTER THE CONVERSATION

Having a good discussion to talk about expectations and shared philosophies before the school year starts is only the first step in forming a good co-teaching relationship. After having that initial conversation, both parties need to follow through with the plan. That may mean that the special education teacher puts together a "cheat sheet" of information on the students with disabilities—highlighting goals, accommodations, and needs—to share with the general education teacher. It could be that the general education teacher gathers curriculum materials to share with the special education teacher, to help him or her gain a firmer grasp of the content.

In addition to "action items," teachers need to feel comfortable continuing or revisiting this initial conversation about co-teaching. Classroom policies that both parties agreed to may look good on paper, but once the co-teachers meet the students it could be that policies need to change. Co-teachers should schedule a "check in" time to address any lingering questions they did not raise in the first conversations and to revisit their approach to co-teaching after meeting the students. It is unlikely that the co-teaching pair will change its philosophy or general approach, but co-teachers may find, for instance, that the students have such academic range that the Parallel Teaching model or the Station Teaching model would be better than the model the pair originally felt comfortable with. All good teachers engage in continual reflection to improve their teaching, and co-teaching pairs are no different. See Chapter 12 for more information on the reflection process.

# Lesson Plan Organizer

| | |
|---|---|
| **Identification of the class** | Subject:<br>Time frame (min. and period):<br>Grade:<br>Number of students: |
| **National or state standards**<br>(Write out relevant parts of the relevant standard.) | |
| **Rationale for instruction**<br>(State rationale given to students for how this instruction may benefit them—write in student language.) | Topic:<br>Rationale: |
| **Daily objectives**<br>(State in operational, measurable terms; objective should be directly linked to evaluation procedures. If you are working with a small group or one-to-one, individual goals may be appropriate; 1–3 goals per lesson.) | Students will be able to: |
| **Individualized education program (IEP) goals/ objectives and accommodations/modifications** | |

Adapted by permission from Kristin Sayeski.

In *How to Co-Teach: A Guide for General and Special Educators* by Elizabeth A. Potts & Lori A. Howard (2011, Paul H. Brookes Publishing Co., Inc.)

| | Notes: |
|---|---|
| **Co-teaching considerations for accommodations/modifications** | *Did we . . .*<br>– Address any non–content-related IEP goals<br>– Address appropriate content-related IEP goals<br>– Consider needs of individual students for assignments and classwork<br>– Discuss how to provide accommodations/ modifications without alienating students with disabilities |
| **Evaluation/monitoring**<br>(Description of how you will evaluate student achievement of lesson objectives; attach any quizzes, questions used for assessment, or worksheets.) | |
| **Instructional sequence**<br>(Estimate amount of time per section.)<br>**Start of class period** (10 min.)<br>Required tasks<br>Collection of homework<br>Warm-up activity | Level of instruction (acquisition, practice, or generalization): |

*(continued)*

Adapted by permission from Kristin Sayeski.

In *How to Co-Teach: A Guide for General and Special Educators* by Elizabeth A. Potts & Lori A. Howard (2011, Paul H. Brookes Publishing Co., Inc.).

**Beginning lesson (intro or connecting to previous day)** (10 min.)
Motivation/relevance
Overview
Directions
Purpose of lesson

**Middle** (20 min.)
Objective
Key questions
Students engaged
Activity
Student sharing
Informal check for understanding

**Closing** (10 min.)
Wrap up
Review of key points
Collection of papers/materials

**Ending of class period**
Required tasks
Collection of classwork

**Materials/equipment/preparation**
(List materials, attach any worksheets or assessment forms, and list web sites needed.)

Adapted by permission from Kristin Sayeski.
In *How to Co-Teach: A Guide for General and Special Educators* by Elizabeth A. Potts & Lori A. Howard (2011, Paul H. Brookes Publishing Co., Inc.)

| Co-teaching considerations<br>(Who teaches what? Who prepares what? Who is responsible for grading which assignments?) | Did we plan for . . .<br>– Seating<br>– Roles in instruction<br>– Roles in discipline<br>– Classroom movement patterns<br><br>Instructional strategies<br>Did we consider including . . .<br>– Mnemonics<br>– Graphic organizers<br>– Cooperative learning strategies<br>– Progress monitoring<br>– Peer-assisted learning strategies | Notes: |
|---|---|---|
| Reflections<br>(Do we need other resources? Will we be using the paraeducator? How will we know we have succeeded?) | Things to consider: | |

Adapted by permission from Kristin Sayeski.

In *How to Co-Teach: A Guide for General and Special Educators* by Elizabeth A. Potts & Lori A. Howard (2011, Paul H. Brookes Publishing Co., Inc.)

## SECTIONS III AND IV OF THE BOOK

Co-planning is the crux of a good co-teaching experience for the teachers and for the students. After the initial getting-to-know-you conversations, co-teachers will need to address details of the teaching process. Given that, the next two sections of this book are laid out to provide information and guidance related to conversations about items in the Co-Teaching Planning Checklist on page 68 and on the accompanying DVD. We encourage co-teachers to use the checklist as they prepare to work together, prepare unit plans, and prepare specific lessons, and we suggest that it would be helpful for both teachers to reflect on Chapters 7–12 together as they cycle through the planning process. Use the checklist often, and use the text as a resource for the discussions you have when determining how best to work together. In addition, please see the Lesson Plan Organizer on pages 72–75 and on the accompanying DVD; this template can be used when planning together.

Chapter 7 provides background information on assessment, helping the teachers develop common language for discussions about how to incorporate formative and summative assessment into their plans. The Co-Teaching Planning Checklist focuses teachers to take the information from Chapter 8, which defines and provides examples of accommodations and modifications, and consider incorporating those items into their shared classroom.

Chapter 9 directs teachers to think about classroom management issues, which co-teachers need to address with each other and with the students from the beginning of the year, but also revisit throughout the year to refine and update practices. Chapters 10 and 11 provide some common background related to effective instructional practices. Though co-teaching itself has not been proven to be either effective or ineffective for improving student achievement, there are a host of research-based instructional strategies that co-teachers can incorporate into their teaching, strategies that will help not only students with disabilities but all students succeed in the co-taught classroom. These chapters separate topics generally by grade, recognizing that the needs and realities of middle and high school students differ from those of elementary students.

It is important that co-teachers cooperatively think about the items in Sections III and IV of this text as they are embarking on a co-teaching partnership. When you are teaching by yourself, you make some of these decisions and policies and planning decisions either on the fly or subconsciously, but in a co-teaching team both parties need to be involved. It takes a conscious, purposeful discussion to formulate agreements on these issues and start off the co-teaching relationship on a good note.

## CONCLUSION

The initial discussion between co-teachers can be difficult if the newly assigned pair do not know where to begin the conversation. The Co-Teaching Planning Checklist provides a framework for the discussion the pair needs to have related to classroom policies and practices, and specifically planning for lessons. Sections III and IV of the book provide additional information related to specific topics on the checklist. What are some topics for discussion as you and your co-teacher talk about embarking on a co-teaching adventure?

 ## REFLECTIONS

- Spend some time outlining what you need to talk about with your co-teacher in the initial discussions. Consider items that may not have been included in this chapter, if there are circumstances unique to your situation.

# III

# Focus on Classroom Teaching

# Assessment to Guide Instruction and Grading

Once you have read this chapter, you should be able to

- Describe formative and summative assessment and when each is appropriate.
- Identify nontraditional ways to assess students' knowledge and skills.
- Discuss with your co-teacher your philosophy on grading and decide your philosophy together.

 *WHAT'S ON THE DVD?*

Ed and MJ talk about how they make grading transparent between themselves and the students.

**WHAT SHOULD I WATCH FOR ON THE DVD?**

- How does Ed and MJ's practice help students succeed? How does Ed and MJ's practice reflect their philosophy that the class is *their* shared class?

## FORMATIVE AND SUMMATIVE ASSESSMENT

Just as meteorologists use different instruments to give them information about different facets of the weather, teachers use different types of assessment to provide them with various kinds of information about a student's knowledge and skills. The two basic types of assessment are formative and summative assessment, and teachers need to use both, depending on their purpose in assessing. Most teachers will have strong background knowledge related to formative and summative assessment before co-teaching. This chapter provides co-teachers with common language and understanding of the multiple purposes of assessment to guide their discussions about how they will assess their students.

*Summative assessments* attempt to *sum up* a student's achievement and knowledge in one sitting, in an attempt to determine what a student knows about a subject after instruction has been completed (Spinelli, 2006). Though these assessments are important in the grand scale of education, the format, timing, and content of these assessments are often dictated to teachers by their local or state school system. Teachers can use summative assessment results to measure their own effectiveness at teaching the content and to demonstrate a student's growth in knowledge over a long period of time. General education teachers are likely to be the "expert" on summative assessment within the co-teaching relationship, because they are more knowledgeable about the content included on summative assessments.

*Formative assessment* involves gathering information about students' performance as they work toward a goal (Spinelli, 2006) and then using that information to *inform* instruction. In summative assessment, the review comes after all instruction; however, in formative assessment the teacher gains insight into student progress as the student is learning. This provides the teacher the opportunity to change instruction if students are not on track to meet an instructional goal or to change the goal if students have caught on more quickly than the teacher originally planned for. When teachers take frequent, informal assessments of student knowledge and use that information to adjust instruction, student performance on summative assessment, and presumably achievement and knowledge, increases (McMillan, 2003). Instructional adjustments in a co-teaching classroom can include, as in a class taught by a single teacher, increasing use of certain in-

---

| BOX **7.1** | **Examples of formative assessment** |

- Warm ups at the beginning of class
- Exit slips before leaving class
- "Mad Minute"—students answer math facts in a timed format, providing a fluency and an accuracy measure
- Observation and questioning
- Checks for understanding

---

structional strategies, altering the content or method of instruction, and providing more support. The benefit of using formative assessment in a co-taught class is that the special education teacher has more training in remediation and altering instruction for students who are not making progress, and students with and without disabilities can benefit from these ideas.

Both formative and summative assessments are important. Summative assessments provide a measure of progress or mastery of long-term goals and can be used to demonstrate end-of-the-road ability in broad-based goals such as achieving sixth-grade math competency. Formative assessments provide a more minute picture, focused on small-level skills or knowledge, and provide teachers the ability to analyze progress toward short-term goals such as achieving competency in two-digit-by-two-digit multiplication. Formative assessment is used to fine-tune instruction as we teach the skills so that students have greater success on summative assessment. See Box 7.1 for examples of ways to incorporate formative assessment into your co-taught classroom routine.

## ASSESSING IN A VARIETY OF FORMATS

Traditionally, assessment took the form of pencil-and-paper quizzes and tests and, though teachers may have always done some informal assessment through observation and questioning, teachers based reported grades on traditional assessments. Over time, the educational culture has started to place greater value on nontraditional assessments, and teachers have turned to the following: *authentic assessments,* which simulate real-life activities; *dynamic assessments,* which assess students during the instructional process to inform instruction; *performance assessments,* which require the students to apply knowledge and use skills; and *portfolio assessments,* a collection of work samples that show students' progress over time (Spinelli, 2006). See Box 7.2 for sample objectives for each of these types of assessment. It is important for co-teachers to consider using a variety of formats for assessment because not all students can adequately demonstrate their

---

BOX **7.2** | **Sample assessments and objectives**

*Authentic assessments:* Given a mock salary, students will research information and create a budget to encompass living and entertainment expenses
for a year.
   *Dynamic assessments:* Given a list of vocabulary words, students will
match the word to the definition using learned mnemonic strategies.
   *Performance assessments:* Given objects of varying lengths, students
will use appropriate tools to measure the objects in both English and metric
systems.
   *Portfolio assessments:* Given a writing prompt, students will write responses with increasing complexity and length over a semester.

---

understanding and skill on traditional assessments. In addition, it may be
easier to differentiate the assessment activity or rubric if using a nontraditional format (see the Negotiating Different Grading Philosophies section
later in this chapter).

A large challenge for assessing students with less mild disabilities in a
co-taught classroom is finding ways to incorporate the assessment of a modified curriculum in the context of a general education class. As discussed
in Chapter 2, federal law requires that schools measure student progress
on their curricular goals, regardless of whether a student might have a disability. What this means in a co-taught classroom is that co-teachers will
often need to assess students working on a modified curriculum sitting
right next to students working on the general curriculum. With careful
planning, co-teachers can create assessments that honor standard course
content while emphasizing alternate curricular goals for some students. See
Box 7.3 for examples of aligning assessments for students on general and
modified curricula.

## GRADING

It is often difficult for teachers to develop grading habits that satisfy their
own needs, and when two people are working together the decisions about
grading policies are made more difficult. However, it is also more important that the co-teaching pair think through grading policies, practices, and
guidelines prior to enacting them so that students see the co-teachers as
equal partners and get consistent answers from both teachers.

As indicated in the Co-Teaching Planning Checklist on page 68 and on
the accompanying DVD, grading issues that co-teachers need to discuss and
resolve differences about include who will do the grading, whether all students will be graded using the same methods, how to grade objectively, and
how to deal with homework.

When considering who will do the bulk, or perhaps all, of the grading, it is important to keep in mind the format of the assessment and the

---

**BOX 7.3**  **Aligning assessments for students on general and modified curricula**

Co-teachers should consider the following when determining how to align assessments:

- Think outside the curricular lines; find the overlap between how you assess the general curriculum and the skills students on a modified curriculum are learning. *Example:* Students on the general curriculum create event cards for a timeline writing details about an historic event that they have to know. A student on modified curriculum puts the timeline in order using the dates.

- Change criteria for a common assessment. *Example:* When students give oral reports on biographies of famous Americans, most are assessed on the content of their report and research, but a student on a modified curriculum uses more supports for the creation of the report and is assessed on oral communication skills.

- Create common assessment time, even when a common assessment is not possible. *Example:* When most students are completing a formative assessment probe on general curriculum content, giving a paper assessment to students on a modified curriculum will enable the students to blend in with the rest of the class.

---

expertise required to check it and provide feedback. If the assessment is a very open format, with room for multiple acceptable answers and interpretation, it may be that the general education teacher, as content expert, will have to score assessments, because he or she has greater understanding of the material. Likewise, if feedback is going to be detailed and require depth of content, such as with a literature essay, the general education teacher, or a content-wise special education teacher, will need to provide the comments. However, if assessments are objective, or if both co-teachers have appropriate content knowledge either because of their background or because they have been teaching together for a long time, either party can do the grading. In such a case, division of labor may come down to who has the most time. We encourage the special education teacher to be involved in grading, when possible, as it keeps a "finger on the pulse" of the class.

An additional consideration when discussing grading duties is the format of the grade book. Some grading programs only allow teachers to have access to "their" students, meaning that the general education teacher could not input grades for the students with disabilities and the special education teacher could not input grades for students not receiving special education services. If distribution of grading, down to the task of recording grades, will be shared equally, co-teachers will need access to the complete student roster. Co-teachers can petition the administration to allow both teachers to have access to both rosters or they can create a shared spreadsheet file on a password-protected school or Internet server and transfer final grades to the roster at the end of each semester.

## Rubrics

Use of rubrics is a best practice in nontraditional assessment, designed to make transparent to students how an assignment or task will be assessed and what the teacher expects (Spinelli, 2006). Rubrics outline criteria and can be used by the student as a checklist while completing an assignment and by the teacher while assessing the assignment. Rubrics provide teachers in an inclusion class a great opportunity to account for individual needs by adjusting the rubric to reflect the needs of individual students. For example, the general class rubric for a paper on the causes of the Civil War may concentrate on quality and quantity of causes, with a small number of points designated for grammar, spelling, and so on. The co-teachers may decide to adjust the rubric for certain students with disabilities. Because the students will be responsible for less information, to earn full points the students have lower criteria. Or the co-teachers may decide to adjust the rubric to focus on writing goals from the IEP, such that the students would be assessed

---

**High school physics application project**

**Purpose:** The purpose of this assignment is to have students create a simple machine (incline plane, lever) and to demonstrate their machine to the class. This demonstration should address how the machine performs "work" and how Newton's First Law of Motion can be applied. Students will be able to describe the principles of Newton's First Law of Motion, apply the principle during the demonstration, and show how the simple machine performs "work." Students will also be able to write a three-page summary of their project, including an example of the equation related to "work" applied to a "real world" problem. The solution to the equation must also be provided.

**Equation:** Work = Force × Distance

**Assignment:** Students will be asked to pull out a slip of paper from the assignment basket. (A selection of simple machines will be on slips of paper.) Once the simple machine has been identified, students will be given class time to research and build their simple machine.
1.  Students will construct their simple machine.
2.  Students will be required to demonstrate their machine to the entire class. Demonstrations should not exceed 10 minutes. During the presentation, please address the following:
    *   Explain how the machine performs work.
    *   Describe Newton's First Law of Motion.
    *   Show how Newton's First Law can be applied to your machine.
3.  Students will prepare a three-page summary of the project, including an example of the equation for "work" using a real-world application. The equation must be solved. Please use the PIES mnemonic to demonstrate the steps in solving the equation. Please use appropriate spelling and grammar in your writing.
The summary should also provide a description of Newton's First Law of Motion with an example. Newton's First Law of Motion (also known as Law of Inertia) states the following:
*   An object at rest will remain at rest.
*   An object in motion will remain in motion at a constant velocity unless acted upon by an external force.

**Grading rubric:** Projects will be graded using the attached rubric. Please review this rubric before submitting your paper for grading.

---

**Figure 7.1.**  Sample high school physics differentiated rubric. (*Key:* PIES, picture, information, equations, and solution.) (*Note:* Italics is used in the adapted rubric to show changes from the original rubric.)

---

**High school physics application project grading rubric**

Name:_____    Total:_____ **150 Points**

**Simple machine**                                               _____ **50**
How is the construction? (Is it sturdy? What materials were used?)
How is the appearance? (How does it look? Colors, graphics)
Does it work?
Is the student's name on the machine?

**Demonstration**                                               _____ **50**
Did the student demonstrate how the machine worked?
Did the student describe Newton's First Law of Motion accurately?
Did the student show how Newton's First Law can be applied to the machine?
Did the demonstration not exceed 10 minutes?
Overall impression of demonstration (Was it well paced? Was it engaging?)
How was the presenter's style (eye contact, speaking style)?

**Summary**                                                     _____ **50**
Did it describe Newton's First Law of Motion accurately?
Did it include the "work" equation?
Did it include a "real world" example of the "work" equation?
Did it include the PIES mnemonic to solve the "work" equation?
Was it three pages?
Did it use correct spelling/grammar/punctuation?

**Comments:**

---

**High school physics application project adapted grading rubric**

Name:_____    Total:_____ **150 Points**

**Simple machine**                                               _____ **50**
How is the construction? (Is it sturdy? What materials were used?)
How is the appearance? (How does it look? Colors, graphics)
Does it work?
Is the student's name on the machine?
*(Note:* For some students, a drawing can replace the actual construction of the machine.)

**Demonstration**                                               _____ **50**
Did the student describe Newton's First Law of Motion accurately?
Did the student show how Newton's First Law can be applied to the machine?
*Did the demonstration not exceed 6 minutes?*
*Did the student present orally?*
*Did the student make eye contact with audience?*
*(Note:* For some students, technology may be used for the demonstration. They could create a slideshow or a short video. Consider how the student may be using assistive technology.)

**Summary**                                                     _____ **50**
Did it describe Newton's First Law of Motion accurately?
Did it include the "work" equation?
Did it include the PIES mnemonic to solve the "work" equation?
*Was it one page?*
Did it use correct spelling/grammar/punctuation?

**Comments:**

---

on general writing and not on content. The purpose of differentiating rubrics is to assess with the most precision and accuracy the specific objectives a student is working on with each assignment. See Figure 7.1 for an example of a differentiated rubric used for a high school physics assignment.

## Homework

Questions regarding homework that co-teachers must resolve together for the students in both general education and special education include what and how much to give, what the purpose of homework actually is, how to grade the homework, and if they will approach homework differently for the different populations. The question of *purpose* is where the discussion between co-teachers needs to begin; in other words, why are you giving this homework? Teachers can assign homework for 10 reasons, as summarized by Epstein and Van Voorhis, "practice, preparation, participation, personal development, parent–child relations, parent–teacher communications, peer interactions, policy public relations, and punishment" (2001, p. 181), though consensus is that using homework as punishment should be completely avoided.

Once co-teachers have agreed on why they are assigning homework, they can answer the questions of what and how much to give. If you use homework to review old content in preparation for end-of-year assessments, then perhaps something that would take 15 minutes twice a week is sufficient. If you use homework to reinforce just-learned skills that students are not yet using with automaticity, then perhaps you should assign homework every day so that students get constant practice. Research on the impact of homework on achievement is mixed, but there is evidence that shows a positive correlation between the amount of time a student spends doing homework—up to a certain point that varies by age and is not a hard-and-fast number—and academic achievement (Marzano & Pickering, 2007).

The question of how to grade homework is the more sensitive issue. Teachers can grade for completion or based on correctness; they can assign homework a great deal of weight in the student's overall grade or can leave homework out of the final grade equation. Whether you grade on completion or correctness may depend on your purpose in assigning the homework. If this is practice of a not-yet-mastered skill, shouldn't the attempt hold more value than the precision? If using homework for formative assessment of previously learned skills, though, teachers need to track accuracy in some way. Some teachers argue that if homework is not calculated into the grade, students will be less motivated to complete it, whereas others suggest that because summative assessments will be evaluating the same skills, grading homework "double counts" a student's performance in a given skill area.

Co-teachers will not need to come to agreement on some homework issues if the school has set policies concerning homework and how homework will be graded. However, most co-teaching pairs will work out homework details before assigning any. Respect each others' perspectives, and remember that not all homework has to be the same or be graded the same.

## Negotiating Different Grading Philosophies

Teachers hold strong opinions about decisions they have made, especially in regards to areas such as grading, where there may be no right or wrong, just opinion and previous experiences. As with any delicate negotiation, co-teachers need to enter the grading discussion with a willingness to compromise and be open to rationales and ideas they have not previously considered or have previously dismissed. Box 7.4 summarizes points co-teachers should consider when deciding on their grading practice.

---

**BOX 7.4 Grading practice considerations**

- **Differential grading**—assessing students on different objectives or with different weights on different assignments

    *Pros:* It assesses the specific objectives each student is working on and accounts for a wide variety of functional levels while allowing students to work on the same task.

    *Cons:* It requires greater organization and gives the perception of lack of fairness.

- **Weighted grading**—calculating grades such that some assignments or assessments count more, or carry greater weight, in the final grade than others

    *Pros:* It can account for the fact that some assignments take more time and require more effort than others; it can put greater emphasis on summative assessments, which reflect achievement, than tasks such as homework, which may be scored for completion.

    *Cons:* It is not as transparent to the students and parents and requires additional compromise and consideration between co-teachers as to how to weight the grades.

- **Zero as a grade**—giving students who do not turn in work zeros to mimic the responsibility that life will require of them

    *Pros:* Students need to complete the task. A zero does not reflect the student's performance on the task, rather a lack of compliance. Continue to give the student opportunities to submit the task, with consequences.

    *Cons:* A zero on missing assignments weighs too heavily against the achievement students demonstrate on completed tasks, so instead of assigning zeros to missing assignments, assign 50 points or 66 points.

- **Accepting late work**—allowing students to turn in work after the due date

    *Pros:* If the purpose of the work was for practice or assessment, the purpose is still met. It encourages students to complete assignments, even if not on the teachers' timetable.

    *Cons:* It sets a precedent against following rules; additional time may be seen as unfair to students who submitted on time, and teachers may end up "chasing" missing grades.

---

## CONCLUSION

Assessment should provide teachers with the information they need to provide effective instruction for all students in their classroom. Co-teachers
need to discuss with each other grading and assessment practices so that
the policies are clear to both the teachers and the students. General education teachers need to be open to using different assessments and grading
methods for different students, and special education teachers need to facilitate that differentiation.

 ***REFLECTIONS***

- What is your philosophy of grading in relation to the items listed in
  Box 7.4?
- What do you see as the purpose of homework? How does that inform
  your classroom practice?

 ***CONNECTIONS***

Experienced co-teachers

- How have you used formative assessment in the past? How can you
  foresee using it in your co-taught class?

Beginning co-teachers

- Did you and your co-teacher plan homework practices together?
  Take some time to reevaluate how well your homework practices are
  working.

Prospective co-teachers

- How will you talk about your grading philosophy with your co-teacher?
  How will you lobby to come to agreement if he or she has a different
  philosophy?

# 8

# Accommodations and Modifications

---

**CHAPTER CHECKLIST**

Once you have read this chapter, you should be able to

○ Define and summarize reasons for providing accommodations and modifications.

○ Describe important factors when considering accommodations and modifications.

○ List examples of assessment accommodations.

○ Discuss with your co-teacher how you will manage accommodations and modifications within your co-taught classroom.

---

 *WHAT'S ON THE DVD?*

---

Sherry and Craig talk about how they adjust instruction to meet the needs of students by limiting the curriculum and providing accommodations in the large group.

 *WHAT SHOULD I WATCH FOR ON THE DVD?*

---

• What accommodations does this co-teaching team provide?

## DEFINITION AND PURPOSE

Chapter 2 provided a very brief definition of accommodation and modification. To reiterate, an *accommodation* is a small change from the norm designed to give a student access to the general education curriculum or assessment as if he or she did not have a disability—for instance, providing additional testing time for a student with a processing disorder. The key to providing an appropriate accommodation is focusing on the last part of that definition: *as if he or she did not have a disability.* Accommodations do not change the curriculum or requirements to enable students with disabilities to perform better than their peers without disabilities; rather, they level the playing field and prevent a student's disability from hindering his or her ability to learn or to demonstrate knowledge.

*Modifications,* or adaptations, however, alter the curriculum that a student is responsible for or the skills on which a student is being assessed. So, instead of being enabled to perform as if he or she does not have a disability, the student is given different criteria for success. An example would be modifying the science curriculum so that the student is responsible for only a portion of the content, such as requiring the student on modified curriculum to be able to recite Newton's Three Laws of Motion, while requiring those on the standard curriculum to conquer this objective and also be able to write and use the corresponding velocity equations. Typically, it is individuals with intellectual disabilities who receive modifications; students with more mild disabilities are more easily able to use the general curriculum—with appropriate accommodations—and will require fewer modifications than those with more severe disabilities. Though the two terms are sometimes used interchangeably, accommodations and modifications really are different constructs, and we discuss them separately in the following sections.

It is important to note that people who are not familiar with the purpose and intentions of accommodations and modifications—for example, some teachers, parents, students, and administrators—often think it is unfair to provide a student with an accommodation or modification. However, it is helpful to adopt the mindset that *what is fair is not that everyone gets the same thing but that everyone gets what he or she needs.* A student who needs a curricular modification cannot successfully learn using the general curriculum due to his or her disability, making it necessary to alter the curriculum in a way that the student can be successful. Would it be educationally fair to provide a modification for everyone, which would mean giving a typically developing student (see Box 8.1 for a discussion of the term *typically developing*) a curriculum he or she has already mastered? Of course not, because not all students have the same educational needs.

IEP teams also should remember that there are ramifications for making the decision to alter the curriculum that the student is responsible for. The vast majority of students with disabilities will be required to take the standard state-mandated accountability assessment, even if the IEP team has

---

BOX **8.1** | **Vocabulary: typically developing**

Though educators most often use the term *students without disabilities* to talk about the counterpart to students with disabilities, there are synonyms for this population. *Typically developing* places emphasis on the fundamental difference between the developmental functional level of students with and without disabilities. A student with a disability has not developed in the traditional, standard, or typical way. Students without disabilities have developed in a statistically average way; therefore, they are typically developing.

---

decided to make modifications to the curriculum. That means that a student could remember everything he or she has learned and perform perfectly on the assessment items related to the curriculum for which he or she was responsible but could still fail the state assessment. Furthermore, because (as discussed in Chapter 2) state assessments may be used to measure a teacher's effectiveness, co-teachers may be hesitant to suggest curriculum modifications. Remember, regardless of the professional ramifications for the co-teachers, if the IEP team decides that a modified curriculum is appropriate, the co-teachers *must* honor the decisions as stated on the legal IEP document.

## ACCOMMODATIONS

A counter to the point of view that accommodations are unfair is that a well-chosen and appropriate accommodation should make no or almost no impact on the performance of a student who does not require the accommodation while eliminating the impact of the disability on the performance of the student with a disability. For instance, the argument goes, a student who has a disability in the area of processing may require more time to complete assignments. If the teacher provides the same accommodation to all students, there should be little or no impact for students who are typically developing and the student with the processing disability should perform better. It is true that multiple studies incorporating various accommodations and ranging the grade levels have found that students without disabilities do not benefit, and sometimes do poorly, when receiving accommodations that their peers with disabilities need (e.g., Elliott, Kratochwill, & McKevitt, 2001; Fletcher et al., 2009; Meloy, Deville, & Frisbie, 2002). However, given that a student without a disability is not "cheating" or getting an unfair advantage over a student who truly needs the accommodation, one could argue that there is merit in providing all students in a co-taught class with accommodations during general instruction and assessment, especially when the accommodation is one that students will use individually (i.e., a student can have a calculator available but not use it if it is not needed; tests can be untimed, but those who do not need extra time will not use it). In fact, providing certain accommodations for an entire

---

**BOX** **8.2** | **Vocabulary: universal design**

---

According to Mace (as cited by Center for Universal Design), *universal design* is "the design of products and environments to be usable by all people, to the greatest extent possible, without the need for adaptation or specialized design" (2008, Paragraph 1). Such products and environments were originally designed for people with physical disabilities (e.g., accessible ramps at building entrances or street-level entrances, automatic doors, curb ramps) but are useful to those without disabilities (e.g., people with strollers, people on bikes, people carrying many items). The concept is also applicable to classroom instructional and assessment environments (e.g., providing a variety of assessment options that will play to students' strengths and allow for "built-in" accommodations, repeating material in a variety of ways, using multimedia in lessons).

---

class aligns with the principles of universal design (see Box 8.2) and does not require that students with disabilities be singled out from their peers.

Along with general concerns about ostracizing students among their peers, it is important that co-teachers try not to single out students as having or requiring accommodations and modifications because students' disability status and IEP are confidential. Instead, the co-teachers need to develop subtle ways of ensuring that they provide appropriate accommodations. If some students are getting an adapted assessment with more white space and additional prompts, for example, take care to hand out the assessments at the same time and in the same manner as if they were all the same. Do not have one teacher hand out the standard assessment and the other hand out the accommodated assessment, as this will draw attention to the differences. Similarly, teachers should casually and covertly hand out calculators to the students who require them, for example, instead of asking students to raise their hands if they have this accommodation. For such purposes, you can take advantage of having two teachers in the room; if using the One Teach, One Assist model, the teacher who is assisting can hand out tools and adapted materials while circling the room. In addition, if students with similar needs are working together during station teaching, teachers can provide accommodations and modifications without typically developing peers being aware at all.

## Assessment Accommodations

Assessment can be broken down into three different, but sometimes overlapping, types: classroom, large-scale, and high-stakes. *Classroom assessments* are given by a single teacher for formative or summative purposes (see Chapter 7). *Large-scale assessments* are given to a large number of students, possibly countywide, statewide, or even nationwide. For *high-stakes assessments,* often given on a large scale, results are used for student promotion;

teacher evaluation; or district, state, or national progress measures. Though each of these assessments serves a different purpose, it is important to consider the same types of accommodations for each assessment. It is not appropriate to provide a student with an accommodation on a high-stakes assessment that he or she is not using regularly in the classroom (Edgemon, Jablonski, & Lloyd, 2006). In addition, IEP teams need to be aware of what accommodations are allowed on high-stakes assessments, as state and district policies about permissible accommodations have, since 2001, focused less on allowing the student to perform as if he or she did not have a disability and more on ensuring that the assessment measures the skills it was originally designed to measure (Lazarus, Thurlow, Lail, & Christensen, 2009). For instance, some high-stakes assessments do not allow a read-aloud accommodation for a reading assessment because it changes the skill being measured from reading comprehension or decoding to listening comprehension.

Accommodation types for assessment include five categories: presentation, time, setting, response, and aid (Edgemon et al., 2006).

1.  *Presentation*—alters the way that the assessment is presented to the student (e.g., questions being read out loud or appearing in large print)
2.  *Time*—changes the amount of time or adjusts the format of the time a student has to complete the assessment (e.g., extended time or breaks in the assessment schedule)
3.  *Setting*—involves some change to the physical environment (e.g., small group, special lighting)
4.  *Response*—allows students to present their responses in a nontraditional format (e.g., dictating to a scribe, marking answers in the test booklet, using a computer or word processor)
5.  *Aid*—provides a student with a physical device to help him or her during the assessment (e.g., use of a calculator, use of a masking device)

Though we encourage you to provide some accommodations to the entire co-taught class on a regular basis, such as reading aloud all assessments so that students who require that accommodation do not have to leave the room, it is important for the IEP team—and both co-teachers as part of that team—to carefully consider what accommodations are appropriate for each student with a disability on large-scale and high-stakes assessments. Not all accommodations are allowed on all assessments, and not all accommodations are appropriate for all students. See Figure 8.1 for a suggested decision-making process for IEP teams assigning assessment accommodations.

Co-teaching teams need to consider how all forms of assessment will be accommodated prior to the beginning of the school year. IEP team decisions related to what accommodations students will use on a high-stakes assessment will drive some decisions about what individual students will require during traditional test and quiz classroom assessment, but co-teachers

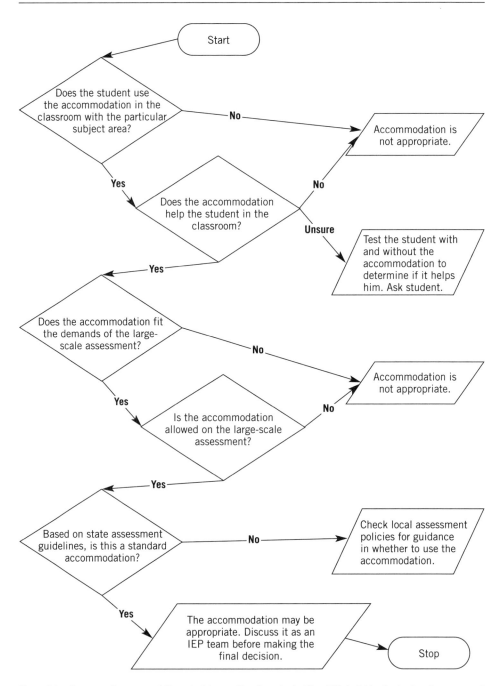

**Figure 8.1.** Assessment accommodations decision-making flow chart. (*Key:* IEP, individualized education program.) (From Edgemon, E.A., Jablonski, B.R., & Lloyd, J.W. [2006]. Large-scale assessments: A teacher's guide to making decisions about accommodations. *TEACHING Exceptional Children, 38*[3], 10; reprinted by permission. Copyright © 2006 by the Council for Exceptional Children, Inc. www.cec.sped.org. All rights reserved.)

have flexibility in how to apply those accommodations to in-class assessment. For instance, as mentioned previously in this section, maybe the team will decide to make an accommodation a standard practice in its classroom by allowing everyone to use calculators, by providing simplified directions for everyone, or by not officially timing assessments. Co-teachers also need to talk about how they will handle the accommodations that they will not apply universally. Who will take the students to their small group? If some students require more time, how will the teachers handle that with the rest of the class?

One piece of classroom assessment that has been left out of the conversation thus far is homework. Chapter 7 discussed the importance of the co-teachers being united regarding homework practices and purpose; providing accommodations for homework is another area co-teachers will need to address before the school year begins. There may be students who require homework to be adjusted in length or content. It may be natural to assume that the special education teacher will take the lead in making any accommodations or modifications, but the general education teacher needs to be involved, too, especially when the special education teacher may not have strong content knowledge. It could be that in accommodating the homework to meet IEP requirements for length, the special education teacher needs guidance on what the most important curricular pieces are so as not to inadvertently omit the main purpose of the homework.

## Instructional Accommodations

Instructional accommodations can overlap with assessment accommodations in nature and use. If a student is using a calculator as an instructional accommodation for completing word problems, it is good practice for that accommodation to carry over into the assessment setting. However, *instructional accommodations* can be more broadly defined to encompass changes to standard instructional methods to meet the needs of the students. With this wide net, teachers who use good instructional strategies based on individual student needs are providing instructional accommodations. A partial list of potential instructional accommodations includes the following, all of which are natural adjustments to most experienced teachers who value differentiating instruction for their students (see Box 8.3 for more on differentiating instruction):

- Use index cards to record major themes
- Give alternatives to long written reports (e.g., write several short reports, preview new audiovisual materials and write a short review, give an oral report on an assigned topic)
- Keep extra supplies of classroom materials (pencils, books) on hand
- Check progress and provide feedback often in the first few minutes of each assignment
- Provide as much time as is needed to complete a task. (PACER Center, 2003, pp. 72–73).

Instructional accommodations in the form of effective instructional practices are very important and are discussed further in Chapters 10 and 11.

---

BOX **8.3** | **Differentiating instruction**

---

Teachers use differentiated instruction when they provide opportunities for students based on their individual needs, interests, strengths, and weaknesses. Examples include the following (Tomlinson, 1999):

- *Learning contracts*, which outline a variety of academic tasks and require the student to negotiate with the teachers which tasks he or she will complete, allowing student choice and catering to different skill levels based on the tasks that each student takes on
- *Tiered activities*, varying the level of abstractness and complexity for different skill levels
- *Learning centers or stations*, which allow students to work on the same objective in a variety of ways

## CURRICULUM MODIFICATIONS AND INDIVIDUALIZED EDUCATION PROGRAM GOALS

Curricular modifications, or adaptations, are not very common in a general education setting. Soukup, Wehmeyer, Bashinski, and Bovaird (2007) observed that students with intellectual and developmental disabilities who were highly included in a general education classroom were only working on an adapted curriculum 18% of the time. For this 18%, it is important to find ways to make connections and find overlap between the general and modified curriculum. This will make the students feel more like they are working on the same things as their peers and will also help the co-teachers with pacing. See Table 8.1 for examples of overlapping adapted curricular objectives with standard state objectives.

What is more important, when serving students with disabilities in a co-taught classroom, is that *all of their instructional needs are being met*, including instructional needs related to IEP goals. Every student who receives special education services has an IEP, and every student's IEP should include instructional goals but may also include goals related to nonacademic skills. It is the legal responsibility of both the special education and the general education teachers to ensure that these goals are addressed wherever the student receives instruction.

Therefore, co-teachers need to look at all pieces of an IEP and determine how they will address the IEP goals within the context of the general education curriculum and classroom demands. The special education teacher will probably take the lead on this task because it is his or her area of expertise, but the general education teacher will play an important role in identifying overlap between opportunities to work on IEP goals and general curricular goals. For instance, if a student has IEP goals related to social skills and working with others, it will be important to provide that student with opportunities to work with his or her peers through cooperative learning activities, group discussions, or group projects. Co-teachers need to plan

**Table 8.1.**  Overlapping adapted curricular objectives with standard state objectives

| Grade-level standard | Alternate standard | Classroom application |
|---|---|---|
| U.S. history: "describing key events and the roles of key individuals in the American Revolution, with emphasis on George Washington, Benjamin Franklin . . ." | Grade 1 history: "describe the stories of American leaders and their contributions to our country, with emphasis on George Washington, Benjamin Franklin . . ." | Overlap the study of these leaders, with different students responsible for researching different aspects of the leaders' lives |
| Earth science: "key concepts include processes of soil development" | Grade 3 science: "understand the major components of soil, its origin, and importance . . ." | Overlap the major concept, with alternate standard presenting review and background for grade-level standard and grade-level standard presenting enrichment for alternate standard |
| Grade 11 English: "write in a variety of forms, with an emphasis on persuasion" | Grade 4 English: "write effective narratives, poems, and explanations" | Overlap a writing topic or prompt with different types of writing: the general topic is cafeteria food, with grade-level standard persuading for more options and alternate standard focused on explaining the present state |

*Note:* This chart uses Virginia Standards of Learning. The grade-level standard is the general curriculum standard for a specific course and the alternate standard reflects a standard from a lower grade level.

*Source:* Virginia Department of Education (2008).

these opportunities so that the student with the disability will be successful and not academically outcast. It may be helpful to assign the students roles, matching the student with the disability to a role based on strengths and abilities. For instance, a student who is good at speaking but not good at writing or analyzing may have the duty to report on the group's work. The co-teachers need to work together to ensure that there are plenty of opportunities to learn, apply, and generalize skills.

## CONCLUSION

This discussion of accommodations and modifications encompasses only a tiny amount of the overall information available, but it should be enough to introduce you to the basics and give you common knowledge with your co-teacher. Can you describe the differences between accommodations and modifications and explain why each is necessary? Can you describe important considerations for providing accommodations and modifications and list some instructional and assessment accommodations? Are you ready to discuss with your co-teacher how you will manage accommodations and modifications within your co-taught classroom?

 *REFLECTIONS*

- What accommodations have you used in the past? What are your general thoughts about accommodations?
- What are you general thoughts, feelings, and biases toward curriculum modifications?

## CONNECTIONS

Experienced co-teachers

- What accommodations do your current students require? Is there a way to provide those accommodations that avoids singling out students with disabilities?

Beginning co-teachers

- How much have you incorporated universal design into your class-room? Identify new ways to meet the needs of all students in your co-taught classroom.

Prospective co-teachers

- Identify ways to differentiate topics for your students.
- What accommodations can you provide to the whole class?

# IV

# Build
# Student Success

# Let's Teach!

## CHAPTER CHECKLIST

Once you have read this chapter, you should be able to

- ○ Describe how you and your co-teacher will arrange your classroom.
- ○ Identify specific instructional tasks that each teacher will be responsible for.
- ○ Create a classroom management plan for all of the students in your classroom.
- ○ Describe how you and your co-teacher will preplan for absences.

 *WHAT'S ON THE DVD?*

MJ and Ed give advice related to what co-teachers need to talk about before the school year begins.

 *WHAT SHOULD I WATCH FOR ON THE DVD?*

- • Have you and your co-teacher talked about the things that Ed and MJ list?
- • How would you have handled the situation that Ed describes with his previous co-teacher and the student who was chewing gum?
- • Do you have a syllabus for your class? Does it reflect the ideas Ed talked about?

## OVERVIEW

In previous chapters we discussed communication, co-planning time, and foundations of co-teaching. Now is the time to discuss the "nuts and bolts" or logistics of teaching in a co-taught classroom. What will each teacher do during a lesson? Who will be responsible for ensuring students are on task? How will the teachers demonstrate their parity or authority to the students? What will happen if one of the teachers becomes ill and cannot come to school? Co-teachers must discuss these questions. In many situations, the answers will change over the school year and as the co-teachers become more comfortable teaching together.

After having the conversations described in Chapter 6, which should provide background and trust-building for the teachers, it becomes evident that the two co-teachers must begin to address the details of how the classroom will be set up and how the teachers will perform instruction together. When possible, given the time constraints of co-teaching, it is helpful to have an idea of each co-teacher's *teaching beliefs* (see Chapter 4). These beliefs are often expressed in how classroom logistics are managed. It is vital that each co-teacher respects and values different perspectives, thus providing a framework to resolve potential areas of disagreement (Friend & Cook, 2007).

In previous chapters, the focus has been on how co-teaching pairs need to build their team; the actual teamwork begins now! Co-teachers must make decisions on the following considerations:

- How will the classroom environment (both physical and social) support our instruction?
- How will each teacher function in the classroom? What will our roles be?
- How will we manage the behavior of the students?
- What happens if one (or both) of us gets sick or needs to be out of the classroom?

## CLASSROOM ENVIRONMENT

Arranging the classroom space is one of the first tasks for any teacher preparing for the start of school. This is also one of the first tasks for the co-teaching team. How should the desks be arranged—in rows, a circle, groups? Each teacher will have preferences, and these preferences can lead to lengthy discussions.

Preferences are important; however, there are practical considerations. In the elementary school classroom, co-teachers should consider traffic patterns and whether they want to use a center-based instructional focus (deBettencourt & Howard, 2007). When considering centers (often used in the early elementary classroom), how easy will it be for students to rotate through the centers? Where will the cubbies be in relation to the centers? Will the centers' locations create difficulties when students are asked to line up to exit the classroom? In the elementary classroom, other considerations might include location of the classroom bathroom, student supplies, and classroom pets. Co-teachers might also want to discuss who will be responsible for the care and feeding of the classroom pets.

In middle or high school classrooms, the considerations may be more related to what content and strategies the co-teachers will be using. For example, if the co-teachers plan to use mostly cooperative learning or group work, it may be best to group desks or tables either in circles or where students can face each other. In some math or science classes, students may be assigned a partner. In these classes, desks or tables may be arranged so that partners can sit next to each other. Again, the co-teachers should recognize the practical considerations of room size; location of door; location of computer, projector, or SMART Board; location of chalkboards or whiteboards; and materials (computers, science labs) that students may need. One additional consideration in middle and high school is that the general education teacher may want a different classroom set-up for other class periods or that the co-teaching team may be in the classroom only for one period and another teacher "owns" that classroom. If the co-taught classroom will require that desks be moved, teachers will need to consider when, how, and who will move the desks at the start of the period and back to their original configuration at the end of the period.

Co-teachers need to decide how the space will be arranged, but they must also consider how they will communicate with the students that both teachers are responsible for the class. For example, teachers need to ensure that both teachers' names are on the classroom door or blackboard (or whiteboard). See Box 9.1 for suggestions on areas that co-teachers should address.

## CLASSROOM CLIMATE

Another element of the classroom environment is related to how students and teachers will interact. This is related to the classroom climate that the co-teachers want to foster. What social climate do the teachers want? Will the students be encouraged to help each other? Will polite manners be required? Teachers at all grade levels will need to decide how they want the classroom to function (Marzano, 2003). More important, they will need to model desired behaviors as much as possible, for the students and with each other.

These behaviors can be as simple as using "please" and "thank you" with both students and the co-teacher. Teachers should make a conscious decision about how they will address their co-teacher (e.g., the same as they expect students to address them), and they probably need to address this before teaching their first class together. This might also include a discussion about how much information about personal or private lives the teachers are comfortable sharing in front of the class. Obviously, some information should not be shared with students; however, during the course

---

**BOX 9.1  Classroom considerations for co-teachers**

Physical layout of classroom (deBettencourt & Howard, 2007)

- How will you arrange desks and tables? Will the desks be in rows or in groups?
- Will you use assigned seating?
- Can you see all of the students from different points in the room?
- Where will you place teachers' desks?
- Can all of the students see the blackboard, video monitor, and teachers' desks?
- How can you ensure ease of movement around the classroom?
- Will certain items or places be off limits or by invitation only?
- Where will often-used materials or books be kept?
- What types of items do you want on the walls?

Co-teacher responsibilities

- Who will ensure that both teachers' names are on the door, on the blackboard, and on all materials that are handed out or sent home?
- Who is responsible for classroom bulletin boards or materials for the walls?
- Will you share materials (markers, pens, paperclips) or will each teacher have his or her own set of supplies?
- How will you ensure that each teacher has private space for personal items (purse, laptop)?
- How does each teacher feel about his or her desk? Can items on the desk be shared or is the desk off limits?

---

of a school year, students may hear about a family pet, coffee drinking habits, or lunch preferences. Co-teachers should communicate their preferences regarding this type of classroom interaction with each other.

Modeling desired behavior can become complicated when it involves identifying or correcting a mistake a co-teacher makes. For example, what happens in math class when one teacher makes a mistake when working a problem? Does the co-teacher have permission to interrupt and correct the mistake? Or, does the mistaken co-teacher prefer that the issue be discussed privately before clarifying with the class? It is not acceptable teaching practice for the teachers to never correct the error for the students! There must be a correction, but the co-teaching issue is how and when the correction occurs. For example, imagine that the co-teachers are teaching a math lesson on long division and the teacher at the blackboard is demonstrating how the number 54 can be divided by 5. The teacher works out the division and comes up with 10, forgetting to show the remainder of 4. The co-teacher realizes the mistake and politely prompts the other teacher to remember the remainder. This can also be an excellent learning opportunity about how everyone can make mistakes and how important it is to fix them.

Co-teachers need to consider how these types of interactions will affect the classroom climate because students will be observing and taking cues from the teachers. For example, if the interruption is polite (e.g., "remember the remainder," students will see respect between the teachers. However, if the interruption is rude (e.g., "you're wrong" or "Mr. S. isn't good at math"), students will see a lack of respect between the teachers. Both of these situations will help to create the classroom climate.

Even in the ideal co-teaching relationship, there will be occasions when there is tension or anger between the co-teachers (or with a student). Most teachers can maintain a professional demeanor; however, in a co-taught classroom any tension between the teachers (or even with specific students) may contribute to the overall classroom climate. All co-teaching teams have relationship ups and downs, such as arguing about a misplaced stapler, a disagreement about how to respond to a parent's e-mail, too much time spent on a lesson activity, and many others that might cause friction between the two teachers. When discussing the classroom environment, co-teachers may want to briefly discuss strategies for managing themselves when this situation happens. Co-teachers may want to have a prearranged signal so that the other teacher can adapt instruction, redirect a student, or provide a "breather" for the stressed teacher. The prearranged signal might be a simple hand gesture for time out or a specific code word or phrase such as "I saw Dan." Although these incidents may vary, it is important to pre-plan how the co-teachers will manage the situation.

Some co-teaching teams have begun to experiment with a new technology that aids communication between them in the classroom. Both teachers are fitted with lapel microphones and earbuds so that they can softly talk to each other while moving around the classroom. Although this approach is still in the experimental phase, some co-teachers report that they like being able to enhance their instruction and communication while assisting individual students. Teachers have been able to quickly redirect students, change their location in the classroom, and even make suggestions to each other in a seamless manner.

On a slightly different topic, one of the advantages to co-teaching is that two teachers are in the classroom. This does provide the opportunity for a teacher to have a bathroom break during class, or for one teacher to take over should the other have a coughing fit or need to run out to make last-minute copies. Although this should not be an everyday practice, there are times when such a break may be needed. Co-teachers may want to pre-plan and develop a code word or signal for this situation, too.

## TEACHER ROLES

In Chapter 1, we described the models of co-teaching: One Teach, One Observe; One Teach, One Assist; Station Teaching; Parallel Teaching; Alternative

Teaching; and Team Teaching. Co-teachers must decide what each teacher will be doing during the lesson (Friend & Cook, 2007). Will one teacher take attendance and move around the classroom assisting students? Will one teacher always be responsible for the collection of homework or the warm-up at the start of the lesson? When students are working independently, will one or both teachers move around the room checking their work? Who will be responsible for which part of the lesson?

Again, co-teachers may find the Co-Teaching Planning Checklist (see page 68 and the accompanying DVD) to be helpful as they make these decisions. The examples of a co-taught elementary lesson plan in Chapter 10 and a co-taught high school lesson plan in Chapter 11 also provide guidance for decision making. These decisions may change over the course of the school year as the relationship develops or as the instructional needs of the students vary.

The logistics of how the classroom and lesson are conducted are important; however, both teachers need to have expertise in delivering instruction to the whole class. This can be challenging for a special education teacher

---

**BOX 9.2 SCREAM mnemonic**

Mastropieri and Scruggs (2010) provided a mnemonic to help teachers (and co-teachers) stay focused on effective instruction. They described the importance of teaching systematically using the following:

- *Structure*—This is a reminder that lessons should be organized with a stated goal or objective, students need to have a preview of the lesson and transition points, and teachers need to review or summarize lessons as they are taught.

- *Clarity*—This is a reminder that teachers need to be clear and concise in their teaching of materials. Avoid confusing language and examples. Strive to communicate effectively with all students.

- *Redundancy*—This is a reminder that teachers need to provide multiple opportunities for students to practice skills and learn new concepts. Most concepts or skills should be taught with multiple examples and through a variety of ways (visual, verbal, hands-on practice).

- *Enthusiasm*—This is a reminder that teachers need to be enthusiastic in their teaching. Remember, if you are bored teaching a lesson, students are bored, too!

- *Appropriate rate*—This is a reminder about how to pace your lessons. To encourage students to focus their attention on a lesson, we recommend a brisk pace of teaching, but the pace cannot be faster than the students can learn. Teachers should actively question students to ensure that the pace of the lesson is not too fast or too slow.

- *Maximize engagement*—This is a reminder that students need to be engaged (on task) during the lesson. Co-teachers can help to manage off-task behavior by moving around the classroom, providing prompts, and questioning students.

who is often responsible for individual or small-group instruction. To successfully teach together, both teachers need to have confidence and ability in teaching (or instructing) the class. Each teacher must be capable of providing an introduction to the lesson, providing guided and independent practice, and informally checking that the students understand the material.

Co-teachers must coordinate their individual teaching styles to ensure that they present a teaching team that maximizes learning for all students. Often, co-teachers find that they need time to learn how to teach together. For example, when is it appropriate for one teacher to interject a comment? It is important to recognize that teaching together requires practice.

Good instruction will help the *entire class* succeed academically. Some instructional strategies (mnemonics, graphic organizers) are effective with all of the students in an inclusion classroom. These strategies will be further discussed in Chapters 10 and 11. Both teachers should focus on effective instruction. Both teachers must manage their instruction to ensure that the variables associated with effective teaching are addressed. The mnemonic SCREAM is used to help remember these variables, described more thoroughly in Box 9.2.

In a co-taught classroom, both teachers are responsible for all of the students. Whereas each of the co-teachers may have a distinct role, both teachers need to view the students as "our students." It is important that the class not become polarized into an "us versus them" environment, as that undermines the purpose and intent of inclusion. See Box 9.3 for suggestions for creating classroom unity.

---

**BOX 9.3 "My" versus "our" students**

It is common to hear a teacher refer to "my students"; however, this designation creates difficulties in the co-taught classroom. Consider a situation in which a special education teacher uses "my students" to refer to students with disabilities and the general education teacher uses "my students" to refer to students without disabilities. The co-teachers have created an "us versus them" feeling within the classroom. Sometimes this feeling can be amplified because an individual teacher may be protective of "his" or "her" students. For example, the special education teacher may provide too much help to students with disabilities during a small group activity or the general education teacher may require writing assignments to meet specific curriculum goals.

Because both co-teachers are responsible for all of the students, how can the us-versus-them class be avoided? Consider the following:

- Refer to the class as "our class."
- Think of all of the students as "our students."
- If possible, have a single class roster for attendance or grading.
- Make an effort to learn every student's name at the beginning of the year.
- Be self-aware. Recognize when you feel protective of a student and communicate with your co-teacher.

## CLASSROOM AND BEHAVIOR MANAGEMENT

In Chapter 6, we gave co-teachers guidance on having "the conversation" that included details about individual preferences for classroom management. *Classroom management* is often referred to as "traffic control" or "crowd control," as it relates to managing the *whole classroom* (Friend & Cook, 2007). Special education teachers have specific skills and training in *behavior management* of *individual students* (Mastropieri & Scruggs, 2010), which is a different issue than general classroom management. Although teacher preferences need to be discussed, both teachers must recognize that classroom management is a significant factor in student achievement (Marzano, 2003; Wang, Haertel, & Walberg, 1993). Simply, students in well-managed classrooms demonstrate higher academic achievement (Wang et al., 1993).

In addition, a well-managed classroom makes instruction easier for the co-teachers (Marzano, 2003). Each teacher has his or her own individual preferences and style of classroom management, and these must be integrated for the co-teaching team to manage the class (Friend & Cook, 2007). So, once the teachers have discussed classroom management, how will they actually manage the class during a lesson?

It is often said that the "best classroom management is engaging instruction." This statement may be cliché in teaching, but it is true. Students who are highly engaged in the lesson are unlikely to cause management issues. Co-teachers should plan lessons that maximize engagement and teach with enthusiasm—using the concepts from the SCREAM mnemonic (see Box 9.2) can be helpful for this.

Another important component of effective classroom management is how the classroom will function in regard to rules, procedures, and routines (Marzano, 2003). Co-teachers will need to define the rules and how they will be applied. Often teachers consider posting a set of classroom rules on a wall or bulletin board. These should be phrased in an affirmative (or positive) statement (respect yourself and others, be polite) and should be limited in their number. A general guideline for elementary school classrooms is no more than five posted rules. Co-teachers will need to agree on how they will enforce the rules and whether (and what type of) punishment will be used when a rule is not followed. When defining and enforcing rules, co-teachers must present a united front.

Some co-teaching teams consciously or unconsciously take on roles for classroom management. One teacher may be perceived by the students as the "good cop" whereas the other teacher is seen as a disciplinarian or "bad cop." Co-teaching teams must find a balance that works for them and their students. For some teams, it may be most effective to take turns being the bad cop, whereas other teams may prefer to maintain their established roles. Either case may be appropriate, but both teachers must be comfortable with the decision and capable of managing the class.

Often, the teachers will vary in their skill level or preferences for classroom management. Perhaps a more experienced teacher is paired with a less experienced teacher. These co-teachers may struggle to establish parity with their classroom management. Or, one teacher may prefer a more authoritarian approach to classroom management whereas the co-teacher prefers less structure. To be effective, all co-teaching teams must establish common ground for classroom management. *Consistency* is vital to effective classroom management; both teachers must strive to be consistent.

In a co-taught classroom, some students with disabilities may have a behavior plan that was developed as part of their IEP. The special education teacher has specialized knowledge of how to effectively design, implement, and monitor these plans. These plans can include the use of a token system, reinforcers (e.g., stickers, privileges), self-monitoring of specific behaviors, and other related interventions (National Dissemination Center for Children with Disabilities, 2005). Both co-teachers will be responsible for implementing this plan in their classroom, and they may choose to adopt a similar-looking plan for all students so as not to single out the students with disabilities and also as a classroom management strategy. The general education teacher should be completely versed in how the plan is to function and what behaviors are desirable or undesirable. Behavior plans can be complex and are too detailed to fully address in this text; special education teachers have specific knowledge to help the co-teaching team successfully implement and monitor these plans. See Box 9.4 for vocabulary on positive

---

**BOX 9.4 Vocabulary: positive behavioral interventions and supports and functional behavioral assessment**

Generally, *positive behavioral interventions and supports* (PBIS) refers to use of positive behavioral interventions to change student behavior (Individuals with Disabilities Education Improvement Act of 2004, PL 108-446). The purpose of PBIS is to help schools educate all students, including those with behavioral problems, using a range of appropriate services. These types of interventions and supports are often used following a functional behavioral assessment (FBA). The purpose of PBIS is to 1) reduce or eliminate specific behaviors, 2) replace a difficult or problem behavior with a more acceptable behavior, and 3) increase the student's ability to achieve in a classroom and develop personal skills for increased quality of life (National Dissemination Center for Children with Disabilities, 2005).

Once an analysis of the student's behavior (FBA) has been completed, the individualized education program (IEP) team develops a plan for modifying or changing a specific behavior or for reinforcing an emerging behavior. The entire IEP team and any other professional who may have expertise with the student should be involved. Both co-teachers should contribute to developing a plan that can be easily implemented in their classroom.

When conducting an FBA, focus on identifying significant, pupil-specific social, cognitive, and/or environmental factors associated with the occurrence (and nonoccurrence) of specific behaviors (National Dissemination Center for Children with Disabilities, 2005). This broader perspective offers a better understanding of the function or purpose behind student behavior, which can be very useful to both co-teachers.

---

BOX **9.5** **Web site resources on behavior plans**

The following web sites provide information for both teachers and parents on how to create, implement, and monitor behavior plans:

- National Dissemination Center for Children with Disabilities (also known as NICHCY): http://www.nichcy.org/Pages/Home.aspx
- PACER Center (the Minnesota Parent Training and Information Center): http://www.pacer.org/parent/php/php-c79.pdf
- Wrightslaw (provides legal information for parents and teachers of students with special needs): http://www.wrightslaw.com/info/discipl.fab.starin.htm

---

behavioral interventions and supports (PBIS) and Box 9.5 for resources on behavior plans.

Another important aspect of classroom management is data collection to help identify problems and possible solutions (Marzano, 2003). Again, this is an advantage of having two teachers in the classroom. The co-teaching model of One Teach, One Observe allows one teacher time to focus on disruptive behavior and their causes. Both teachers need to collect and jointly analyze data; however, the special education teacher will have specific skills related to data collection.

The team should focus on using an agreed-on process to identify and collect data on classroom behaviors. For example, suppose an elementary school classroom becomes chaotic and one student begins crying. One co-teacher could spend the day observing this particular student. When the teachers review the data, they might find that the student is having difficulty with transitions between work centers. The solution may be to have one of the co-teachers preview transitions with this student. Or, consider a high school classroom where a group of students seems to be off task during classroom discussions. A co-teacher spends time observing these students and notes that the students are not off task but are engaging in private conversations related to the class discussion topic. Both of these situations benefit from the addition of a second teacher in the classroom to help problem solve. See the data collection forms on the accompanying DVD and also see Figure 9.1 for a Behavior Frequency Chart.

Successful co-teaching teams will effectively manage classroom and student behavior with a unified approach. Both teachers are responsible for managing the class to ensure that each lesson fosters student learning. Although co-teachers need to discuss their perspectives on classroom management, the effective team will learn how to work together through teaching and managing the class.

# Behavior Frequency Chart

Student name: _____

Target behavior: _____

*Directions:* Use tally marks to note each occurrence of the target behavior during the designated time period.

| Date | Period 1 Time: | Period 2 Time: | Period 3 Time: | Period 4 Time: | Period 5 Time: | Period 6 Time: |
|------|------|------|------|------|------|------|
|  |  |  |  |  |  |  |
|  |  |  |  |  |  |  |
|  |  |  |  |  |  |  |
|  |  |  |  |  |  |  |
|  |  |  |  |  |  |  |
|  |  |  |  |  |  |  |
|  |  |  |  |  |  |  |
|  |  |  |  |  |  |  |
|  |  |  |  |  |  |  |
|  |  |  |  |  |  |  |
|  |  |  |  |  |  |  |
|  |  |  |  |  |  |  |
|  |  |  |  |  |  |  |
|  |  |  |  |  |  |  |
|  |  |  |  |  |  |  |

**Figure 9.1.** Behavior Frequency Chart. (DEBETTENCOURT, LAURIE U.; HOWARD, LORI, A., EFFECTIVE SPECIAL EDUCATION TEACHER: PRACTICAL GUIDE FOR SUCCESS, THE, 1st Edition, © 2007. p. 130. Reprinted by permission of Pearson Education, Inc., Upper Saddle River, NJ.)

## TEACHER ABSENCES

Teacher absences happen! Teachers get sick. They attend workshops or trainings. Co-teachers will, at some time in the school year, be absent, too. Each co-teaching team should preplan some strategies for when one or both of the co-teachers will be away from the classroom. Sometimes (e.g., absence for a training or other scheduled event), teachers can create a lesson plan and prepare materials so that the instruction can continue without them. In other cases (e.g., absence due to illness), teachers may not have prepared materials or a plan.

The team needs to discuss a few "what ifs" when planning for absences. Consider a situation wherein one teacher is absent and the other co-teacher must teach with a substitute co-teacher. What will the substitute co-teacher do during the lesson? How will "the team" function when the co-teachers may have had little notice that they would teach together on that day? Often, the substitute will need to take direction from the nonabsent co-teacher. The dynamic between the co-teacher and substitute may affect the classroom climate; consequently, the co-teacher may need to emphasize classroom management in these situations.

Another series of issues occurs when there is a long-term absence by one of the co-teachers. An individual substitute teacher may be assigned to fill in for the absent co-teacher over the course of many weeks or even months. In this situation, the nonabsent co-teacher will need to establish a new working relationship with the long-term substitute teacher. The previous advice to co-teachers regarding respecting perspective and discussing preferences should be followed. In developing these temporary teams, both the co-teacher and the substitute need to focus on working together and ensuring student success.

The co-teacher may find forging this new relationship to be emotionally difficult, depending on the relationship between the established co-teachers and the reason for the long-term substitute teacher. For example, what if the absent co-teacher is suffering a life-altering illness? Or, perhaps, the absent co-teacher may have a temporary physical impairment (broken leg, surgical procedure). The nonabsent co-teacher may want to be supportive of the absent co-teacher while also establishing a working relationship with the long-term substitute. It can be both physically and emotionally tiring to juggle these different relationships while teaching.

Co-teachers who are in these situations are gently reminded that respectful communication with both teaching partners may help smooth difficulties. In addition, all co-teachers should ensure that they maintain a balanced perspective, which may be easier when they take time to relax. After all, even co-teachers need to relax and rejuvenate to stay focused on the important task of teaching the student. This is why having a plan for substitutes (or at least a discussion) can be helpful. See Box 9.6 for some suggestions on co-teaching with substitute teachers.

---

**BOX** **9.6** **Substitute teachers: suggestions for co-teachers**

- Welcome them! (They are there to help you.)
- Create a "Substitute" folder or accordion file that has important hints or tips on how the classroom functions. It could also have worksheets or activities that students can do. Give the folder (or file) to the substitute when you meet.
- Create a generic lesson agenda so that the substitute has some idea of how the lesson is going to flow. Place this agenda in the folder or hand it to them.
- Make sure to provide any specific information related to students with special needs (behavior plans, medical needs).
- Ensure that the substitute knows what the lesson is going to be about (curriculum, purpose).
- Ask the substitute about his or her preferences and how the substitute likes to function in the classroom.
- Thank them!

---

## CONCLUSION

After reading this chapter, it should be apparent that the conversations related to co-teaching will be ongoing and detailed. Co-teachers must develop the skills needed to teach a lesson together. This may require changes in how an individual teacher approaches the classroom setup, how instruction will be managed, how the class will be managed, and how the teachers will prepare for their absences from the classroom.

When reviewing the chapter checklist, can you check the items as complete? Have you and your co-teacher had a discussion about how the classroom will be arranged? Do you and your co-teacher know who will be responsible for specific tasks (homework grading, guided practice, making quizzes)? Have you and your co-teacher discussed behavior plans and classroom rules? Do you have a substitute plan in place for when one of you is absent from the classroom?

Teaching an effective lesson together is the essence of co-teaching. It takes planning, discussing, and practicing, but the rewards for both the co-teachers and students can be exciting and positive. A shared lesson that is successful can create the potential for future co-teaching and student success.

 ***REFLECTIONS***

---

- What do you see as your role in the classroom management system?
- What are your ideas about how the classroom should be set up?

**CONNECTIONS**

Experienced co-teachers

- Reflect on your previous years of co-teaching. Is everything working? Is there something you need to change? What lessons have worked well? Where have students had the most difficulty with a specific concept (e.g., learning to tell time, magnetism)?
- If you do not have one, create a plan for substitutes with your co-teacher.

Beginning co-teachers

- Negotiate with your co-teacher to decide on classroom routines and which of you will be responsible for each of the classroom tasks (warm ups, attendance, making copies).

Prospective co-teachers

- Consider with your co-teacher how you will arrange the classroom, what type of classroom climate you want to encourage, and how you will deal with classroom management.

# 10

# Instruction in Elementary Classrooms

---

## CHAPTER CHECKLIST

Once you have read this chapter, you should be able to

- ○ Recognize instructional strategies that support learning for all of your students in the co-taught elementary classroom.
- ○ Identify three instructional strategies that can be used successfully in your classroom.
- ○ Describe the challenges and rewards of creating an inclusive environment in your own classroom.
- ○ Create a co-teaching lesson plan that incorporates instructional strategies for all students as well as accommodations or modifications for students with special needs.

---

 *WHAT'S ON THE DVD?*

Ed and MJ describe, for their active physics class, the mnemonic *PIES*.

**WHAT SHOULD I WATCH FOR ON THE DVD?**

- What co-teaching model are Ed and MJ using in this clip?
- What makes this an effective instructional technique?

Although many aspects of co-teaching are similar across curriculum and grade level, some features are unique to co-teaching in elementary classrooms. Consider that an individual elementary school teacher is responsible for teaching a range of content (reading, math, science, and social studies) and incorporating social skills. A special education teacher may be assigned to a morning class to assist with reading instruction and have a different co-teacher for an afternoon class focused on social studies at a different grade level. A general education teacher may be comfortable individually managing a classroom and have to adapt to having a co-teaching special education partner for a section of a day or only on specific days.

Instructionally, the primary focus of an elementary classroom is the teaching of reading and math. Since 2001, NCLB has also focused teachers on measuring student progress in these areas (U.S. Department of Education, 2005). As time has passed, NCLB has also added science to the areas being measured. As previously discussed, there is an emphasis on student achievement through the use of standardized test scores, and these measures are increasingly being used to evaluate teacher performance.

So, there is an increased focus on standardized testing in the elementary school classroom while more students with special needs are being placed in general education classes. The confluence of these two trends has understandably created tension and anxiety for the general education teacher in the elementary classroom (Patterson & Protheroe, 2000). A special education co-teacher can be sensitive to the concerns related to high-stakes testing by providing instructional strategies to assist with skill development for the entire class. Many strategies that are successfully used by students with special needs (e.g., mnemonics, graphic organizers) are also excellent strategies for all students when learning content-specific material (Mastropieri & Scruggs, 2010).

In addition to the focus on reading and math, elementary school students are learning social skills and the ability to function in a school (e.g., lining up, walking in the hall, raising their hand). There is a vast difference in the abilities of early elementary students (kindergarten and first grade) and late elementary students (fifth and sixth grade) related to maturational or developmental differences. Teachers in elementary schools must recognize these differences and help students learn the necessary skills for school success. In a co-taught class, both teachers must be willing to coach, role model, and define expectations for these skills (e.g., sharing, turn-taking) throughout the day.

## IDENTIFICATION OF STUDENTS NEEDING SPECIAL EDUCATION SERVICES

In an elementary school, all classrooms really are inclusive because students with mild disabilities often are not identified until they are in the elementary grades; many classrooms contain students who have not yet been identified as needing special education but who are struggling to learn (Hallahan, Kauffman, & Pullen, 2009). For a student to qualify for special education services, the student must first be referred to a team of professionals for an assessment; often, the general education teacher makes this referral based on the student's lack of performance or struggles in the classroom. This team of professionals may be called "Child Find" or "the child study team." This group determines whether the classroom teacher has tried interventions with the student and may offer ideas of more things the classroom teacher can try to increase student achievement. Only after the teacher has made multiple attempts to intervene can the student be further assessed and determined eligible for special education services.

Since 2000, there has been increased emphasis on using interventions before referring a student for special education evaluation, leading to the development of *school-based prereferral teams* (also called *student/teacher intervention teams* and *student/teacher assistance teams*). General education teachers consult these teams to identify strategies that might help a student *before* he or she becomes identified as needing special education services (Hallahan, Kauffman, & Pullen, 2009). IDEA 2004 has provided funding for additional classroom interventions for students with suspected learning disabilities before they are eligible for special education services. This idea of trying different interventions before eligibility for services has become known as *response to intervention (RTI)*—if a student responds to low levels of intervention, he or she does not have a disability and is not eligible for services; if a student requires more intense interventions to sustain academic or behavioral growth, he or she does require special education. RTI has expanded the role of the general education teacher in the special education identification process beyond just making a referral to implementing strategies and interventions and collecting data that will be used to see if a student is eligible for special education services. For co-teaching teams, both teachers can be instrumental in identifying strategies that may work for students who are struggling in the classroom. See Box 10.1 for more details on RTI.

## INSTRUCTION

The instruction in a co-taught elementary classroom and a traditional one-teacher classroom looks very similar because the curriculum and the students remain the same. The old adage "good instruction is good instruction for all" is applicable in both classrooms. However, co-teachers should be using specific strategies that have been identified as effective through research (often called *evidence-based strategies*). These are the most effective

---

**BOX** ██**10.1**██ **Response to intervention (RTI)**

According to the National Joint Committee on Learning Disabilities, the underlying rationale for RTI is that, "when provided with quality instruction and remedial services, a student *without* disabilities will make satisfactory progress" (2005, Slide 3). So, teachers should focus on identifying specific strategies that will help struggling students achieve adequate progress. The following are to be in place when implementing an RTI approach:

- High-quality, research-based instruction and behavioral supports in general education
- Scientific, research-based interventions focused specifically on individual student difficulties and delivered with appropriate intensity
- Use of a collaborative approach by school staff for development, implementation, and monitoring of the intervention process
- Data-based documentation reflecting continuous monitoring of student performance and progress during interventions
- Documentation of parent involvement throughout the process (National Joint Committee on Learning Disabilities, 2005, Slide 5)

As more schools implement an RTI approach, general education teachers are being asked to implement evidence-based strategies with struggling learners, while concurrently documenting the student's progress so that a determination of the student's progress can be made. This is in addition to their teaching responsibilities. Co-teaching teams can share this responsibility and knowledge of interventions, thus making RTI more manageable and effective. Some examples of ways to use co-teaching to ease the implementation of RTI include the following (Murawski & Hughes, 2009):

- Using the One Teach, One Observe model, co-teachers can collect data on progress.
- Special educators have additional training and expertise in the interventions that are a part of RTI, so they can ease the planning and implementation.
- Having two teachers automatically lowers the student–teacher ratio and provides greater opportunity to work with students at risk for failing.
- During parallel instruction, groups can be arranged so that students who need interventions receive more intensive instruction.

---

instructional strategies or methods that all teachers should be using and include peer-assisted strategies, mnemonics, and graphic organizers (Forness, Kavale, Blum, & Lloyd, 1997).

Although the following discussion provides an overview of these strategies, please consider the previous chapter on accommodations and modifications that may be needed for students with special needs. These instructional strategies may assist all learners but are not to replace or reduce the need for an individual student's accommodations and/or modifications as detailed on the IEP.

## Cooperative Learning and Peer-Assisted Learning Strategies

In inclusive classrooms, one of the most effective instructional strategies is cooperative learning (Putnam, 1998). *Cooperative learning* occurs when groups (or pairs) of students work together in a learning activity and are all responsible for their own and their groups' learning outcomes. However, to be effective, cooperative learning must be carefully structured to ensure student success (Jacobs, Power, & Loh, 2002). Cooperative learning provides an opportunity for students to work together in a group to complete learning activities (Mastropieri & Scruggs, 2010). When the groups are carefully constructed, this strategy can provide benefits in both academic achievement and social skill development. See Box 10.2 for a discussion on selecting group members for cooperative learning.

As previously mentioned, reading is one of the most important skills that children must master in the elementary years. During reading instruction, students are often grouped by their ability level and use basal readers to practice their reading. In some schools, reading groups are selected gradewide. Some students may be selected to leave their classroom to be a member of a reading group in another classroom. Sometimes, a student

---

**BOX 10.2 Group work considerations**

Co-teachers can assign a group activity or learning experience to focus on content or social skills. It is important to identify the purpose of the group activity before assigning group membership to students. Although it is possible to combine a content and social focus, generally it is better to identify one of the purposes as the focus before creating the assignment. Also, consider mixed-ability groupings when the purpose is social and ability groupings when the purpose is content-related or academic. Remember, most reading and math groups are considered ability groupings, and these groups should not be the only groups students work in.

Teachers need to consider individual learning and personality differences in assigning groups. Group size is another consideration. Sometimes a pairing is most appropriate; however, some projects may benefit from a group of three or four students (Howard & James, 2003). Students with special needs should be included within the groups.

**TEACHER EXERCISE**

Cooperative learning activities can be used in multiple ways in the elementary school classroom. Think of using "shoulder partners" for checking spelling in a writing assignment or asking a group of four students to classify the biodiversity in a specific ecosystem. Some teachers consider what social skills (turn-taking, sharing of materials) they want to promote when they develop a cooperative learning activity.

Can you describe a cooperative learning activity and decide which students should be grouped for the activity? Consider how the group composition changes when the purpose changes. Do you maintain the same group membership when the purpose is social skill development?

with special needs may leave the classroom for individual or small-group reading instruction with a special education or resource room teacher. Members of each group are selected by their reading ability level. In a co-taught classroom, it is important that reading group membership not determine group composition for all group activities, as some groups should be designed to foster social skill development (Johnson & Johnson, 1981; Mastropieri & Scruggs, 2010).

A specific type of cooperative learning is called *Peer-Assisted Learning Strategies* (*PALS*), and this strategy has been proven effective (Fuchs & Fuchs, 2005; Fuchs, Fuchs, & Burish, 2000). In the PALS strategy, students are paired, and the student with the weaker skills in an area (e.g., reading, math) provides a verbal explanation of the math problem or reading concept (Fuchs & Fuchs, 2005). This strategy can benefit both the tutor and the tutee, as it provides both a supportive learning environment for the less experienced student and practice for the more capable student, and because engagement is high for both students.

*Classwide peer tutoring* is another version of peer-assisted learning and is very similar to PALS. The significant difference is that the paired students (tutor, tutee) both take turns leading the instruction. This particular version of peer-assisted learning has been documented to work with all learners in an inclusive classroom and for different content areas (math, reading, social studies) (Mastropieri & Scruggs, 2010). When implementing a classwide peer tutoring program, it is vital to follow a systematic approach in order to be successful. See Fuchs and Fuchs (2005) for a description of how to implement a classwide tutoring program for reading.

## Social Skills and Cooperative Learning

Many elementary school teachers (both general and special education) note that much of the school day is spent teaching social and self-help skills. In the early elementary classroom (kindergarten, first grade), students learn to share their materials (e.g., markers, scissors), to put their coats in their cubbies, to express their emotions (e.g., happy, sad, angry), and to develop friendships with classroom peers. These skills are important to all elementary school students. Cooperative learning opportunities can be designed to foster the development of these skills (Johnson, Maruyama, Johnson, Nelson, & Skon, 1981; Mastropieri & Scruggs, 2010).

When grouping students to promote social skills, it is important that learners with special needs be grouped with their peers without disabilities (Johnson & Johnson, 1986; Mastropieri & Scruggs, 2010). The co-teachers should provide coaching and assistance to help the groups learn to work together. This may include reassuring students that they can ask for help, helping the groups resolve conflicts, and assigning specific students to group roles. Teachers may also assign each member of the group a role or function (e.g., recorder, timekeeper, reviewer) to perform. Each member of the group must be accountable for their participation in the group project, while the teachers move around the room monitoring each group

(Sonnier-York & Stanford, 2002). Both co-teachers should model cooperative (polite) behavior for the students.

## Mnemonics

Memory lapses are a familiar problem. A student cannot remember that Thomas Jefferson wrote the Declaration of Independence. You forget your grocery list and, while at the store, cannot remember that you need milk for your cereal the next morning. A new teacher is introduced at the faculty meeting to the other teachers at her school; the next day in the hallway, the new teacher is greeted by a fourth-grade teacher and cannot remember the other teacher's name.

Most teachers can recall a time that they forgot something and know that students often struggle with remembering facts and information, and teachers can also recall using memory tricks (mnemonics) to help remember things such as the year Columbus came to America ("Columbus sailed the ocean blue in 14-hundred-92"). Understanding memory and how it works is important to all teachers because of the volume of things that students are asked to memorize. Special education teachers have experience and training in specific strategies that can assist students with recalling important information. See Box 10.3 for examples of mnemonics.

---

**BOX 10.3 Mnemonics**

Mnemonics can include using letter strategies such as *acronyms* or *acrostics* to help remember lists of things. Many people are familiar with the *HOMES* acronym as a way to remember the Great Lakes:

- H = Huron
- O = Ontario
- M = Michigan
- E = Erie
- S = Superior

In addition, many people learned the order of the planets in the solar system with the acrostic My Very Efficient Mother Just Served Us Nine Pizzas (Mercury, Venus, Earth, Mars, Jupiter, Saturn, Uranus, Neptune, and Pluto [when Pluto was still considered a planet]). Other mnemonic strategies use visual clues and pictures (keywords) to help remember items.

**TEACHER EXERCISE**

Many examples of mnemonics can be found on the Internet, in textbooks, and in teacher's guides. You may be familiar with *FOIL* (First Outer Inner Last) or *PEMDAS* (Please Excuse My Dear Aunt Sally—parentheses, exponents, multiplication, division, addition, subtraction) in math. Or, you may have used King Phillip Came Over For Green Soup in a biology class for learning kingdom, phylum, class, order, family, genus, species.

Can you create a mnemonic for use in your co-taught classroom?

---

BOX **10.4** Graphic organizers

---

Graphic organizers can be used with a variety of content areas. You may be familiar with the use of the "hamburger" organizer for the teaching of writing. The "top bun" is the opening paragraph of an essay, then there is the "meat" (what the writer needs to convey to the reader), the "lettuce, tomato, pickles" (the garnishes or details to help support the "meat"), and the "bottom bun," the concluding paragraph that finishes the essay.

Or, you may be familiar with the use of "interactive notebooks" in science or social studies, which have key information and visuals pasted into them. One side may have vocabulary words, while the other side may have a visual or graphic that the student must complete with key words. There are also software programs (e.g., Inspiration) that assist students by helping to create a "web" or concept map to visually link content.

**TEACHER EXERCISE**

Many graphic organizers can be found on the Internet, in textbooks, and in teacher's guides. You may be using these already. Can you identify or create a graphic organizer for use in your co-taught classroom?

---

### Graphic Organizers

Graphic organizers are another effective strategy that co-teachers in elementary classrooms can use with all of their students (Mastropieri & Scruggs, 2010). Graphic organizers can be used in all content areas and can help students learn to organize information that needs to be learned or used. You may be familiar with a story map that students complete after reading a book or short story—it can help improve the comprehension of key events (Kim, Vaughn, Wanzek, & Wei, 2004)—but graphic organizers can also be helpful in social studies, science, and even math. The important element of graphic organizers is that they present a *visual* way for students to organize or understand the material. See Box 10.4 for more examples of graphic organizers.

### LESSON PLANNING TOGETHER

As discussed in earlier chapters, co-planning together is vital for the success of the co-teaching team (see the Co-Teaching Planning Checklist on page 68 and the accompanying DVD). Lesson planning (or unit planning) is essential for teachers. There are a myriad ways to plan a lesson (or unit), and many school districts provide a guide or templates for teachers to use related to specific content or curriculum standards. Generally, successful co-taught lesson plans will contain the following (deBettencourt & Howard, 2007):

- The purpose and objective of the lesson
- The state or national standard(s) that will be addressed

- The sequence for instruction that will be used
- The materials (texts, lab equipment) and equipment that will be used
- The evaluation tools (quizzes, homework) that will be used to monitor learning
- The accommodations or modifications that will be needed
- The material each co-teacher will be responsible for teaching, preparing, or grading

See Figure 10.1 for an example of an elementary school co-taught lesson plan. Notice how this lesson plan differs from that of a traditional, single-teacher lesson plan.

With the increased scrutiny and focus on students achieving learning outcomes as measured by high-stakes testing, it has become imperative that both co-teachers remain focused on what is essential for students to learn. One of the best lesson planning methods for achieving this focus is a process known as *backward design* (Wiggins & McTighe, 2005). Using backward design, teachers plan by starting with the state or national standards, think about how students will be assessed on these standards, and create their lesson or unit plans to meet the standards. The idea is to "begin with the end in mind" to ensure that your planning (and instruction) stays focused on what is essential for the learners to know or understand (Wiggins & McTighe, 2005). In a co-taught classroom, the IEP goals of the students with disabilities need to be addressed. A lesson (or unit) planning process that encourages teachers to plan for these goals and accommodations and modifications and integrate them into the curriculum instruction ensures that both co-teachers' responsibilities (content and IEP) are easily incorporated into instruction. See Wiggins and McTighe's *Understanding by Design* (2005) for more detailed information on lesson planning through backward design.

## PROGRESS MONITORING

In a co-taught elementary school classroom, both teachers will need to collect data or information on student progress (see Chapter 7). This information may be needed for formative assessments of student learning or to help determine how students should be assigned to work in groups. The special education teacher needs to collect information on how students with special needs are progressing on their IEP goals. There are many ways to collect this type of information, but there should be agreement as to how often it will be collected, who will collect it, and what type of forms may be needed. In a math class, the co-teachers may decide to collect exit tickets that require each student to work two math problems before dismissal. The team needs to decide who will collect the tickets, note individual student answers (correct or incorrect), and record the data (on a spreadsheet). See pages 132–134 and the accompanying DVD for sample tracking forms. The Seating Chart Progress Monitoring Form is a sample tracking format designed

# Lesson Plan Organizer

| | |
|---|---|
| **Identification of the class** | **Subject:** Social studies (U.S. History)<br>**Time frame (min. and period):** 4th period, 50 minutes<br>**Grade:** Fifth<br>**Number of students:** 23 (inclusion) |
| **National or state standard**<br>(Write out relevant parts of the relevant standard.) | The student will describe colonial America, with emphasis on the factors that led to the founding of the colonies, and key individuals and events in the American Revolution including King George, Lord North, Lord Cornwallis, John Adams, George Washington, Thomas Jefferson, Patrick Henry, and Thomas Paine.<br>(Virginia Standard of Learning: History and Social Science, USI.6, p. 5) |
| **Rationale for instruction**<br>(State rationale given to students for how this instruction may benefit them—write in student language.) | **Topic:** Important people in the American revolution<br>**Rationale:** The purpose of this unit is to identify and understand the roles of key figures in the American Revolution. The differences in the American and British perspectives on the revolution will be explored. |
| **Daily objectives**<br>(State in operational, measurable terms; objective should be directly linked to evaluation procedures. If you are working with a small group or one-to-one, individual goals may be appropriate; 1–3 goals per lesson.) | **Students will be able to:** identify key figures in the American Revolution.<br>Students will be able to examine and describe key facts about figures in the American Revolution.<br>Students will be able to assess and evaluate the impact of key figures on the American Revolution. |

| Individualized education program (IEP) goals/objectives and accommodations/modifications | *Differentiation strategies* |
|---|---|
| | *Students will develop their own KWL charts for key figures. A KWL chart has three columns. The first column is a list of what students KNOW, the second column is a list of what the students WANT to know, and the third column is a list of what the students LEARNED.* |
| | *Students will develop personal learning contracts.* |
| | *Activities will be tiered.* |
| | *Students will have options on how to research key figures: texts, Internet, video.* |
| | *Accommodations* |
| | *Simplified text readings, peer support, extended time, shortened assignments, and other accommodations as stated on IEP* |
| | *List IEP goals* |
| | *1. Oral language goals* |
| | *2. Written anguage goals* |
| | *3. Organizational goals* |
| **Co-teaching considerations for accommodations/modifications** | *Notes:* |
| | *Did we . . .* <br> X Address any non-content–related IEP goals <br> X Address appropriate content-related IEP goals <br> X Consider needs of individual students for assignments and classwork <br> X Discuss how to provide accommodations/modifications without alienating students with disabilities |

**Figure 10.1.** Co-taught lesson plan example for fifth-grade social studies lesson. (Adapted by permission from Kristin Sayeski.)

(continued)

Figure 10.1. *(continued)*

| | |
|---|---|
| **Evaluation/monitoring**<br>(Description of how you will evaluate student achievement of lesson objectives; attach any quizzes, questions used for assessment, or worksheets.) | *Unit test with matching, multiple choice, and short essay question (60 points)*<br>*Test will be 20% of unit grade. Report and presentation (180 points).*<br>*Process: Student group (20 points)*<br>*Report and presentation rubric: Spelling/grammar, logical sequence, critical roles and why, oral skills (50% )*<br>*Write a newspaper article from a Colonial newspaper (20 points). Comment upon support of Revolution, using appropriate spelling/grammar, note key figures (10% of unit grade).*<br>• *Homework completion with be 10% of unit grade.*<br>• *Students will complete an individual KWL chart about each figure.*<br>• *Student rubric KWL chart, spelling/grammar, key events in lives (10% of unit grade)* |
| **Instructional sequence**<br>(Estimate amount of time per section.)<br><br>**Start of class period** (10 min.)<br>Required tasks<br>Collection of homework<br>Warm-up activity | Level of instruction (acquisition, practice, or generalization):<br><br>*Notes: Collect homework (related to reading assignment) and warm up (test-taking prep: two questions with discussion). Go over agenda and lesson objective.* |

128

| | |
|---|---|
| **Beginning lesson (intro or connecting to previous day)** (10 min.)<br>Motivation/relevance<br>Overview<br>Directions<br>Purpose of lesson | Introduce lesson by looking at money (Washington, Jefferson), then talk about monuments in Washington, D.C. Encourage students to discuss what they know—who are these people? Have students been to Mount Vernon? Identify any misconceptions. Introduce concept of obituaries; pass out newspapers with obituaries. Have students review, then go over key points: dates, family, accomplishments, and so forth. Ask students to imagine that they were newspaper writers in Colonial America—what might they want to put into an obituary of a Colonial figure? Use discussion to activate prior knowledge and as an informal zone of proximal development (ZPD) check. (The ZPD is where instruction should be targeted for students to be most effective.) |
| **Middle** (20 min.)<br>Objective<br>Key questions<br>Students engaged<br>Activity<br>Student sharing<br>Informal check for understanding | Guided practice: Teacher begins drafting obituary for George Washington—what was he famous for? What are the key dates he lived? (Have prepared questions to ask students—they may use their textbook.)<br><br>Assign pairs of students a key figure of the American revolution and ask the pairs to identify the key information about the person. Give them resources. They may use their textbooks or the Internet. Both teachers walk around room assisting students as needed. Teachers may need to use proximity to keep students on task. (Teachers may also need to use reminders about staying on task/noise level.) Give time prompts.<br><br>If time permits, have students share key facts with others. If time is short, make sure to build in time next lesson to have the students share what they found about their person. |

*(continued)*

**Figure 10.1.** *(continued)*

| | |
|---|---|
| **Closing** (10 min.)<br>Wrap up<br>Review of key points<br>Collection of papers/materials | Closing routine:<br>Remind students to put materials away (textbook).<br>Review what was learned (may need to define obituary again).<br>Talk about key dates, facts, and accomplishments.<br>Provide any "preview" information that may be required.<br>Collect any materials (newspapers) that may be still on their desks.<br>Exit slip (ask them to write key fact for their assigned person) |
| **Ending of class period**<br>Required tasks<br>Collection of classwork | Begin transition to next lesson |
| **Materials/equipment/preparation**<br>(List materials, attach any worksheets or assessment forms, and list web sites needed.) | Williamsburg video (previously viewed—may link it for prior knowledge)<br>Newspaper (obituary section)<br>Use of Internet for research on key figures |

| | | Notes: |
|---|---|---|
| **Co-teaching considerations** <br> (Who teaches what? Who prepares what? Who is responsible for grading which assignments?) | *Did we plan for . . .* <br> X̲ Seating <br> X̲ Roles in instruction <br> X̲ Roles in discipline <br> X̲ Classroom movement patterns <br><br> Instructional strategies <br> *Did we consider including . . .* <br> X̲ Mnemonics <br> X̲ Graphic organizers <br> X̲ Cooperative learning strategies <br> X̲ Progress monitoring <br> X̲ Peer-Assisted Learning Strategies | *Seating is in place; both teachers will move around classroom during the pair activity (cooperative learning). Special education teacher will introduce lesson and do test-taking warm up. General education teacher will provide guided practice on writing the obituary. Both teachers will move around the room assisting students.* |
| **Reflections** <br> (Do we need other resources? Will we be using the paraeducator? How will we know we have succeeded?) | Things to consider: *What went well? What would I change next time? Do I need to provide more guided practice? How was the noise level? Did the students work well together? Did they meet the objectives? How did we do? Anything to note as we plan the next lesson?* | |

# Seating Chart Progress Monitoring Form

Use this seating chart to monitor student progress. As you ask students questons during class, make notations about their responses. Suggestion: Use tick marks for good answers, circles for missed responses.

*How to Co-Teach: A Guide for General and Special Educators* by Elizabeth A. Potts & Lori A. Howard

# Exit Slip Tracking Form

Use this form to note student progress on daily exit slips. Note correctness of answers and track learning trends.

| Student | Day 1 | Day 2 | Day 3 | Day 4 | Day 5 | Day 6 | Day 7 | Day 8 | Day 9 | Day 10 | Day 11 | Day 12 |
|---------|-------|-------|-------|-------|-------|-------|-------|-------|-------|--------|--------|--------|
|         |       |       |       |       |       |       |       |       |       |        |        |        |
|         |       |       |       |       |       |       |       |       |       |        |        |        |
|         |       |       |       |       |       |       |       |       |       |        |        |        |
|         |       |       |       |       |       |       |       |       |       |        |        |        |
|         |       |       |       |       |       |       |       |       |       |        |        |        |
|         |       |       |       |       |       |       |       |       |       |        |        |        |
|         |       |       |       |       |       |       |       |       |       |        |        |        |
|         |       |       |       |       |       |       |       |       |       |        |        |        |
|         |       |       |       |       |       |       |       |       |       |        |        |        |
|         |       |       |       |       |       |       |       |       |       |        |        |        |
|         |       |       |       |       |       |       |       |       |       |        |        |        |
|         |       |       |       |       |       |       |       |       |       |        |        |        |
|         |       |       |       |       |       |       |       |       |       |        |        |        |
|         |       |       |       |       |       |       |       |       |       |        |        |        |

*How to Co-Teach: A Guide for General and Special Educators* by Elizabeth A. Potts & Lori A. Howard

# Curriculum-Based Measurement Tracking Form

Use this form to note student performance on probes. Probes should contain opportunities (points). Consider graphing the data (or having students graph data) to get a graphic representation of progress.

| Student | Probe 1 | Probe 2 | Probe 3 | Probe 4 | Probe 5 | Probe 6 | Probe 7 | Probe 8 | Probe 9 | Probe 10 | Probe 11 | Probe 12 |
|---|---|---|---|---|---|---|---|---|---|---|---|---|
| | | | | | | | | | | | | |
| | | | | | | | | | | | | |
| | | | | | | | | | | | | |
| | | | | | | | | | | | | |
| | | | | | | | | | | | | |
| | | | | | | | | | | | | |
| | | | | | | | | | | | | |
| | | | | | | | | | | | | |
| | | | | | | | | | | | | |
| | | | | | | | | | | | | |
| | | | | | | | | | | | | |
| | | | | | | | | | | | | |
| | | | | | | | | | | | | |

*How to Co-Teach: A Guide for General and Special Educators* by Elizabeth A. Potts & Lori A. Howard

to provide a format for teachers to take notes on student responses to in-class questions. The Exit Slip Tracking Form will help teachers keep track of student progress as indicated by answers on exit slips. The Curriculum-Based Measurement Tracking Form provides a structure to collect data from curriculum-based measurement. The co-teachers must regularly and consistently address how progress will be monitored, and this can be discussed during co-planning time. However, each team of co-teachers may want to develop its own forms, too.

## WORKING WITH PARENTS

A distinguishing characteristic of the elementary school classroom is the relationship between the co-teachers and parents. Many schools have active parent–teacher organizations that provide fundraising for school events, chaperones for field trips, or parent volunteers in classrooms. In addition, many parents walk or drive their students to school and have daily contact with the child's teacher. Co-teachers need to preplan how they will communicate with parents regularly, at parent–teacher conferences, and informally when the parent may be present in the school. Co-teachers should strive to provide a "united" team in their interactions with all parents.

Ideally, co-teachers will know that they are co-teaching prior to the start of the school year and can plan how they will communicate with parents. Will they send home a weekly note? Will an e-mail or an electronic newsletter be sent to parents? When (and who) will telephone parents and for what reasons? In most cases, teachers may want to alternate who calls the parents so that one teacher is not always "the bearer of poor reports" and also to impress on the parents that both teachers are working with their child, not just the general or special educator. However, there may be situations of family preferences that will require contact with only one teacher. In all of these cases, both teachers need to keep each other informed. Keep in mind that no parent wants to be consistently or regularly telephoned at home to hear about a child's poor performance or behavior. Make sure to telephone parents with positive information about the child, too.

Parent–teacher conferences should also be planned by the co-teachers. Ideally, both co-teachers should be present at conferences with parents; however, given the realities of schedules this may not always be possible. Sometimes a parent will feel an affinity toward one co-teacher and not the other. This can cause tension between the co-teachers; however, if the parent works better with one teacher, it may be helpful to use that when establishing a good relationship with the parent. In all circumstances, the co-teachers should maintain communication with each other and with the parents. It is vital for all co-teachers to strive to establish positive relationships with parents beginning at the start of the school year. See Box 10.5 for some suggestions for Back-to-School Night.

In the elementary school classroom, co-teachers will have multiple challenges for establishing and maintaining positive relationships with

---

**BOX 10.5 Back-to-School Night**

---

One of the first opportunities for interaction with parents is Back-to-School Night. Both co-teachers should plan to be present in the classroom to meet all of the parents. Plan to provide information on the school day and what the students will be learning, and to respond to any parental concerns. Co-teachers should be respectful to each other and to the parents. The partnership should be seen as a team that will work to ensure that all students succeed. Consider how you will convey to parents a sense of equity in the partnership, using signals such as having both teachers' names on the door, comparable positioning of the teacher desks, and including both teachers' names on any handouts or materials to be sent home with the parent.

**CONFIDENTIALITY**

Parents are often curious about their child's classmates; please keep in mind the need to maintain confidentiality.

---

parents. Co-teachers should discuss policies related to birthday party invitations, parent volunteers in the classroom, classwide parties for special events, and field trips. Individual parents may have strong emotional responses to these, and co-teachers should strive to establish equitable policies. For example, often children will invite other classmates to their birthday party. This can become a difficult situation when some students are excluded while others are included in the invitation. Some schools have established policies that if the invitation is distributed in school, then all of the children need to be invited. This type of policy can limit the concerns of parents and reduce the exclusion of specific students (often those with disabilities).

Similarly, many schools have established policies on parent volunteers in the classroom, including training for these parents. Although parents should be welcomed into the co-taught classroom, there should be established boundaries and responsibilities for the parent. In addition, the school policy and training should address the issue of confidentiality for all of the students in the classroom. Parent volunteers may also be recruited for chaperoning field trips. See Box 10.6 for information on field trips logistics for co-teachers.

## CONCLUSION

When reading through this chapter, the elementary co-teacher should have recognized many of the challenges of teaching this population. In a co-taught classroom, many of the challenges are the same as in a traditional classroom; however, there are strategies that teachers can adopt for use

---

**BOX 10.6 Field trips**

---

Field trips provide an excellent way to expand students' experiences with material through visits to museums, zoos, community organizations, and related sites. However, they also present logistical challenges to the co-teaching team. When planning a field trip, carefully consider the following:

1. Where are we going? How long will it take to go from the school to the site and back?

2. How many students will be going? Do not forget to get parent permission slips to parents. How will you follow up with a parent if the slip is not returned quickly?

3. Which co-teacher will coordinate with parents and with the school?

4. Do we need extra help in managing the class? Consider recruiting parent volunteers.

5. Which co-teacher will be responsible for making contact with the site to be visited?

6. How will we prepare the students to maximize learning on the trip?

7. Who will be responsible for keeping a checklist to ensure that all students who should be present at the site are accounted for?

8. Which co-teacher (or both) will be responsible for ensuring that the same number of students who leave for the field trip return to the school? (This is a vital consideration!)

In a co-taught classroom, it is important that all students be included in the field trip. This may present difficulties when some students have behavior that precludes their participation in outings outside of the school building. Any decision to exclude a student from a field trip should be carefully considered through discussion with the parents and school administrators. In many cases, students can be supported so that they can participate in the field trip. In some cases, students may have a successful experience if accompanied by a parent or someone who knows them well. You might ask the parent to attend the field trip.

---

with the entire class. Again, the chapter emphasized the importance of co-planning time and communication between the co-teachers.

When reviewing the chapter checklist, can you check the items as complete? Can you (and your co-teacher) create a co-taught lesson plan? Can you identify students that could be grouped together for a project or activity? Can you list some concerns about your co-taught classroom and possible solutions to try?

 ### *REFLECTIONS*

---

- Which of the strategies discussed in this chapter have you used before? What is your comfort level with each strategy?

- What are some ways that you will establish communication with parents? Will you use a newsletter, e-mail, or weekly notes home?

 **CONNECTIONS**

All co-teachers

- Which co-teacher will take the lead on each strategy?
- Use the Co-Teacher Planning Checklist on page 68 and the accompanying DVD to plan your next lesson.

# 11

# Instruction in Middle and High School

---

## CHAPTER CHECKLIST

Once you have read this chapter, you should be able to

○ Recognize instructional strategies that support learning for all of your students in the co-taught middle or secondary classroom.

○ Identify three strategies that can be used successfully in your classroom.

○ Describe the unique needs of students in a co-taught class related to self-determination and self-advocacy.

○ Create a co-teaching lesson plan that incorporates instructional strategies for all students, as well as accommodations and modifications for students with special needs.

---

 ## WHAT'S ON THE DVD?

Sherry and Craig talk about how they share instructional and planning responsibilities.

**WHAT SHOULD I WATCH FOR ON THE DVD?**

- How do Sherry and Craig's decisions about the split in workload reflect each co-teacher's strengths? How do the decisions reflect each co-teacher's likes and dislikes?
- Do you consider strengths, likes, and dislikes when you and your co-teacher plan?

Co-teaching at the middle and secondary levels shares fundamental characteristics of co-teaching at the elementary level but requires some specific and special considerations. Although *accountability* is a buzz word at all levels of education, the stakes are higher for students in middle and high schools, where failure to achieve can lead to failure to graduate and failure to graduate has long-term effects on life outcomes. Level and pace of content, the expectation that students have independent study skills, high-stakes testing (Mastropieri & Scruggs, 2001), and block scheduling (Dieker & Murawski, 2003) all present unique concerns for secondary inclusive classrooms. In addition, adolescence is a time of physical, hormonal, and emotional changes that affect students' ability to function socially and academically.

## INSTRUCTION

The educational emphasis in middle and high school shifts away from learning *skills* to learning *content,* with the assumption that students have already learned the skills required to acquire content knowledge. Unfortunately, most students with disabilities have not learned the prerequisite skills that will make traditional secondary instruction effective for them. Co-teachers need to be aware of the gap that may exist in student readiness for learning content and be ready to adapt instruction so that all students can learn the content, regardless of their prerequisite skills.

### Effective Instructional Strategies

The instructional strategies described in Chapter 10 are all applicable and equally effective for students in middle and secondary grades. In addition, strategy instruction and content enhancement routines are supported by a great deal of research related to students in the upper grades. *Content enhancement routines* are a structure for learning and lesson planning that is designed to instruct all students, in partnership with the students, and maintains the teacher as the content expert in the classroom while enabling the teacher to manipulate the content to emphasize important pieces (Bulgren, Deshler, & Lenz, 2007). Content enhancement routines draw together the effective teaching practices of providing structure, building on prior knowledge, using graphic organizers, and working collaboratively to manipulate

---

**BOX** **11.1** **Self-regulated strategy development**

*Self-regulated strategy development* is a method for teaching students how to memorize and use a strategy, self-assessing their use as they learn the strategy. Teachers should follow these steps to teach the strategies (De La Paz, 1999):

- *Description*—the teacher describes the strategy for the student, including why he or she needs this strategy and when it will be useful.
- *Activate prior knowledge*—the teacher helps the student make links to skill sets the student has mastered and that he or she will need to perform the strategy.
- *Review current level of performance*—the teacher determines the student's current ability to use the strategy, to gauge where to begin teaching use of the strategy.
- *Model use of strategies*—the teacher demonstrates use of the strategy.
- *Collaborative practice*—the teacher and student practice using the strategy together.
- *Independent practice*—the student practices using the skill alone.
- *Memorize strategy*—the student memorizes the strategy.

---

and generalize information (Bulgren, 2006; Bulgren et al., 2007). Content enhancement routines are effective for secondary co-taught classrooms because they focus on the individual's needs in relation to prior knowledge and provide a great deal of scaffolding to reach each student; they can also be used for any content area and help students reach higher-order thinking skills.

*Strategy instruction* seeks to teach students some of the learning skills they are missing so that they can learn the content more readily; in other words, cognitive strategy instruction seeks to teach students how to think about their learning (Joseph, 2010). Cognitive strategy instruction can be used to teach students how to use any strategy and is best used with other evidence-based strategies such as mnemonics and direct teaching strategies. Teaching these strategies can be accomplished through a variety of means, but the method with the most research behind it involves the principles of *self-regulated strategy development*; see Box 11.1 for a definition and more information on self-regulated strategy development.

## Textbooks

Though textbooks are used across all grade levels, middle and high school teachers tend to rely on them more than elementary school teachers. This increased use of textbooks poses problems for students with disabilities in co-taught classes because often they do not have sufficient background knowledge, cannot use comprehension rules and strategies, or lack the basic reading skills to comprehend the texts we ask them to read for learning

(Brown, Campione, & Day, 1981). Co-teachers need to be aware of which and how many of their students are likely to struggle with comprehending the text and consider adapting the text requirement. Co-teachers should consider providing alternatives to the text, decreasing the amount of material students read so that they only read what is absolutely necessary, or providing structure such as graphic organizers or guiding questions to help increase student comprehension (Dyck & Pemberton, 2002). If providing different levels of support or adaptation for different students, co-teachers should take care not to make the differences in requirements obvious to the students. With two teachers in the classroom, it will be easier both to create or find necessary adapted texts and to distribute differentiated materials without drawing attention to student differences.

### Study Skills and Test Taking

One reason students struggle academically is because of a lack of study skills. Most students, regardless of disability or intelligence, have the same barriers to academic success: the inability to organize self, thoughts, or work. Some students learn study skills more naturally and more quickly than others, and those who have learned how to use these skills are more likely to succeed in school (Berry, Hall, & Gildroy, 2004, as cited in Mastropieri & Scruggs, 2010). The co-taught classroom is a natural place to work on organizational skills because it is likely that students who need instruction in this area include students with and without disabilities.

Along with direct instruction in note-taking and test-taking skills, as described in this section, teachers will find that students need guidance in using other organizational skills. Homework planners are a common sight in middle and high schools, but teachers need to demonstrate how to use the planners. One co-teacher can model what students should write in the planner, while the other circulates to make sure the students are following along. In addition, teachers need to teach students how to break down larger projects into smaller steps and make these smaller steps evident in the homework planner. This same process of modeling is helpful for organization of notes and papers. Keep a sample notebook and a three-ring hole punch handy to demonstrate how students can keep together all of their materials for one class.

Notetaking is a highly valuable study skill, perhaps the one that students will use most often in their school career (Sabornie & deBettencourt, 2004), especially when paired with listening skills. Co-teachers can provide structure for students to prompt and teach them how to improve their note-taking skills within the context of typical instruction. Examples include providing guided notes or partial outlines, teaching students how to use a published note-taking format such as Cornell Notes, and teaching students how to make their own structure (Mastropieri & Scruggs, 2010). Co-teachers can model good note-taking skills as they instruct, with one co-teacher taking notes on an overhead projector while the other provides instruction. During this time, the teachers can model using abbreviations, asking questions for clarification, writing summaries (Mastropieri & Scruggs, 2010), and discriminating important information.

Test-taking skills and some study skills such as listening are more difficult to teach within the context of a co-taught upper-grade classroom. When the majority of students have a skill, it is difficult to spend time on that skill with the large group. However, it may be beneficial to review major test-taking skill ideas with the large group, and it would definitely be worthwhile to find time to cover test-taking skills with those who require the instruction while using Station Teaching or Alternative Teaching models. Important concepts in test-taking skills include teaching students 1) to review and follow the directions, 2) how to manage their time during the assessment, 3) strategies for specific types of questions (e.g., crossing out incorrect choices as they rule them out for multiple choice questions), and 4) to review their answers and check to be sure they followed directions and answered all questions (Steele, 2007). An effective test-taking strategy that can be taught using the strategy instruction steps listed in the previous section is PIRATES (Hughes, Ruhl, Deshler, & Schumaker, 1993), which stands for

- *Prepare* for the test, prepare to succeed
- *Inspect* the instructions
- *Read* each question
- *Answer* or abandon each question
- *Turn* back
- *Estimate* answers for the remaining questions
- *Survey* your test

## LESSON PLANNING

As important as co-planning time is for all grade levels, it is even more important for middle and secondary classes. It is more likely in the upper grades that the special education teacher will not be a content expert and that the general education teacher will have less knowledge and experience with educational accommodations and adaptations and will be less open to having students with disabilities in his or her classroom than are elementary counterparts (Mastropieri & Scruggs, 2001). In addition, it is important that co-teachers consider the impact and possibilities involved if their school is using block scheduling. Dieker and Murawski (2003) suggested that block scheduling may make it easier to provide some accommodations and modifications (especially varying the instructional methods), may create opportunities for teachers to be equal stakeholders (each leads different activities in the same class period to appear more as a team), and may provide opportunities for a special educator to work with more than one general educator in the same class period. As middle and high school co-teachers plan, they should refer to the Co-Teaching Planning Checklist on page 68 and the accompanying DVD and to the general planning guidelines listed throughout the book. See Figure 11.1 for a sample lesson plan for a secondary co-taught class.

# Lesson Plan Organizer

**Identification of the class**

Subject: *Science (Physics)*
Time frame (min. and period): *90 minute period, MWF*
Grade: *Tenth*
Number of students: *21 (6 special education)*

**National or state standard**
(Write out relevant parts of the relevant standard.)

*The student will investigate and understand scientific principles and technological applications of work, force, and motion. Key concepts include*

*a)   speed, velocity, and acceleration;*
*b)   Newton's laws of motion;*
*c)   work, force, mechanical advantage, efficiency, and power; and*
*d)   applications (simple machines, compound machines, powered vehicles, rockets, and restraining devices).*

*(Virginia Standard of Learning: Science, PS.10, p. 26)*

**Rationale for instruction**
(State rationale given to students for how this instruction may benefit them—write in student language.)

Topic: *Newton's Laws of Motion*
Rationale: *The purpose of this lesson is to examine the attributes of the First Law of Motion.*

*First Law of Motion (also known as Law of Inertia)*
*An object at rest will remain at rest*
*An object in motion will remain in motion at a constant velocity unless acted on by an external force.*

| **Daily objectives**<br>(State in operational, measurable terms; objective should be directly linked to evaluation procedures. If you are working with a small group or one-to-one, individual goals may be appropriate; 1–3 goals per lesson.) | Students will be able to:<br>1. *Describe Newton's First Law of Motion.*<br>2. *Identify key components of the law (including vocabulary: inertia, at rest, velocity, force)*<br>3. *Describe the experiment in a lab report (written language skills). The lab report must be written in scientific language, using acceptable science format, and include descriptions of hypothesis, data collection methods, and conclusions. (Sample lab report sections will be handed out as an advanced organizer.)* |
| **Individualized education program (IEP) goals/objectives and accommodations/modifications** | *Differentiation strategies*<br>*Activities will be tiered.*<br>*Partners for lab assignment*<br>*Accommodations*<br>*Simplified text readings, peer support, extended time, shortened assignments, and other accommodations as stated on IEP*<br>*List IEP goals*<br>1. *Oral language goals*<br>2. *Written language goals*<br>3. *Organizational goals*<br>4. *Social skills goals* |

*(continued)*

**Figure 11.1.** Sample upper-grade co-taught lesson plan. (Adapted by permission from Kristin Sayeski.)

Figure 11.1. *(continued)*

| | Notes: |
|---|---|
| **Co-teaching considerations for accommodations/modifications** | *Did we . . .*<br>X Address any non–content-related IEP goals<br>X Address appropriate content-related IEP goals<br>X Consider needs of individual students for assignments and classwork<br>X Discuss how to provide accommodations/modifications without alienating students with disabilities | IEP goals for written language and social skills. (Partners for social skills and lab reports for written language.) |
| **Evaluation/monitoring**<br>(Description of how you will evaluate student achievement of lesson objectives; attach any quizzes, questions used for assessment, or worksheets.) | *Evaluation*<br>Informal check for understanding through discussion and review of homework assignment (reading in text)<br>Informal monitoring during experiment<br>Review of written lab report<br>There will be a summative assessment (a unit test on Newton's Laws). | |
| **Instructional sequence**<br>(Estimate amount of time per section.)<br><br>**Start of class period** (10 min.)<br>Required tasks<br>Collection of homework<br>Warm-up activity | *Level of instruction (acquisition, practice, or generalization):* Acquisition and practice<br><br>Take attendance, review homework, warm up—2 SOL-type questions on whiteboard for students to answer. (5 min. for answers, 5 min. for discussion of strategies on how to select correct answer)<br><br>Review PIES mnemonic: Picture, Information (circle), Equation, Solve it<br><br>Introduce lesson: Ask students about roller coasters. Show PowerPoint on roller coasters. Use discussion to focus on prior knowledge. (15 minutes) | |

| Beginning lesson (intro or connecting to previous day) (10 min.)<br>Motivation/relevance<br>Overview<br>Directions<br>Purpose of lesson | Give instructions for lab experiment. Review safety precautions; ensure that one person will be the scribe and one person will be the experimenter. Remind students that they are to "switch" for the second experiment. Transition students to their lab stations, and ask them to make sure they have all of the required materials.<br><br>Have students begin the experiment—walk around room assisting individual pairs of students as needed (25 minutes). Use experiments designed and available from National Science Teachers Association (http://www.nsta.org). These instructions will be printed out and given to each pair of students. |
|---|---|
| Middle (20 min.)<br>Objective<br>Key questions<br>Students engaged<br>Activity<br>Student sharing<br>Informal check for understanding | Experiment concludes: Instruct students to clean up their lab stations. Ensure students have taken data for their lab report. Have students begin writing their lab reports (15 minutes, independent practice).<br><br>Ask students if there are any questions. Review what was observed during the experiment (guided practice and linkages to help them formulate their conclusion for their lab report). Have students discuss their data or findings. Ask them to tell what happened. Link to vocabulary of inertia, at rest, velocity, and so forth (15 minutes). |
| Closing (10 min.)<br>Wrap up<br>Review of key points<br>Collection of papers/materials | Closing routine<br>1. Reminder about upcoming homework (reading assignments, problems to work)<br>2. Reminder about upcoming unit test<br>3. Any other reminders<br>4. Ask students if they have any questions about homework or experiment<br>5. Hand out exit problem to work on (basic force velocity equation that students must problem-solve and turn in as leaving class). Use mnemonic PIES. |

*(continued)*

**Figure 11.1.** *(continued)*

| | |
|---|---|
| **Ending of class period**<br>Required tasks<br>Collection of classwork | |
| **Materials/equipment/preparation**<br>(List materials, attach any worksheets or assessment forms, and list web sites needed.) | *Experiment materials (ball, inclined plane)*<br>*Worksheet with guided practice for lab report*<br>*PowerPoint slides for roller coasters*<br>*Exit slips with equation* |
| **Co-teaching considerations**<br>(Who teaches what? Who prepares what? Who is responsible for grading which assignments?) | *Did we plan for . . .*<br>X Seating<br>X Roles in instruction<br>X Roles in discipline<br>X Classroom movement patterns<br><br>Instructional strategies<br>*Did we consider including . . .*<br>X Mnemonics<br>X Graphic organizers<br>X Cooperative learning strategies<br>X Progress monitoring<br>X Peer-Assisted Learning Strategies<br><br>*Notes:* |
| **Reflections**<br>(Do we need other resources? Will we be using the paraeducator? How will we know we have succeeded?) | *Make sure to review article on teaching science to students with learning disabilities (Grumbine & Alden, 2006).*<br>*Check exit slips and homework to assess whether the students understood the First Law of Motion.* |

## TRANSITION

Though teachers and parents should be thinking about post–high-school goals for students very early in their lives, the bulk of planning for life after high school will occur in the middle and high school years. IDEA 2004 requires that all students with disabilities have formal transition plans by the time they are 16, placing the issue of transition firmly in the hands of middle and high school IEP teams. What this means for a traditional co-teaching team of a general educator and special educator teaching a general curriculum content course is that it is likely that students with more severe disabilities will be included in these courses less often as they progress through the grades because these students will be receiving services in more practical skills and spending time at job sites and learning job skills. Students with milder disabilities will continue to receive services in a co-taught classroom but will have additional IEP goals related to postsecondary employment, education, living skills, and community participation. If students receive all of their services in the general education classroom, co-teachers will need to ensure that there is opportunity to work toward those goals in the context of class.

### Self-Determination

*Self-determination* involves setting goals and working to meet those goals and includes subskills of choice making, decision making, problem solving, goal setting and attainment, self-observation and evaluation, self-instruction, and self-awareness, among others (Wehmeyer, Agran, & Hughes, 1998). Many middle and high school students, not just those with disabilities, struggle with these skills. Incorporating opportunities for students to learn and practice these skills in their typical school day will be beneficial to all of the students in the classroom (Konrad, Fowler, Walker, Test, & Wood, 2007). See Box 11.2 for examples of how to incorporate self-determination instruction into the co-taught classroom.

---

**BOX 11.2 Self-determination in the co-taught class**

- Provide students opportunities to make choices, perhaps by requiring that they complete one of two assignments.
- Provide checklists for multiple-step assignments and projects and teach students how to use the checklists to self-assess.
- Provide students with guidance and opportunity to break up long-term assignments and set goals for completion of each step. See Konrad, Walker, Fowler, Test, and Wood (2008) for a detailed discussion of how to plan for inclusion of self-determination in the general education classroom.

Both the general education teacher and the special education teacher should be involved in the development of IEP goals and objectives, as discussed in Chapter 2, which can include skills such as self-determination. One way to continually work on self-determination is to include the student in the IEP process (McGahee, Mason, Wallace, & Jones, 2001). Students who are in co-taught classrooms can work on self-determination skills within the context of large-group instruction. Writing activities, for example, can be molded to give students the opportunity to explore their long-term life goals.

## Self-Advocacy

Self-advocacy is a subset of self-determination but carries enough importance to address as a separate topic. *Self-advocacy* is the act of speaking up for or defending oneself (Wehmeyer et al., 1998). This skill becomes vitally important through the middle and high school years, because teachers begin to coddle students less as they get older and to expect students to ask for help if they need it. Students with disabilities who are in a co-taught classroom tend to be more academically inclined than those in self-contained or pull-out classes and, therefore, are more likely than students with disabilities in other settings to go on to postsecondary education. It is vital that they are able to identify when they need assistance and then persist in obtaining that assistance. In postsecondary schools and in the workplace, individuals with disabilities have rights that they may need to assert to avoid discrimination or to obtain necessary accommodations. Without good self-advocacy skills, students will not be able to be independently successful in college (Smith, English, & Vasek, 2002) or the workplace. See Box 11.3 for ways co-teachers can support self-advocacy.

---

**BOX 11.3** **Self-advocacy in the co-taught class**

- Teach students their rights. In a history or government class, teachers can talk about disability rights—and how they translate to a postsecondary setting—during a civil rights unit.
- As an individualized education program (IEP) team, decide when and how much it is appropriate for students to be "in charge" of requesting their accommodations. Older students will be well served by having responsibility for making sure they receive their accommodations.
- As classroom policy, require students to ask for help.
- In literature lessons, use a book containing a main character with disabilities and have students advocate for the character in a writing activity (Konrad, Helf, & Itoi, 2007).

---

| BOX **11.4** | **Incorporating transition individualized education program (IEP) goals into content instruction** |

*IEP goal:* The student will understand credit, proper use, and the consequences of improper use.

- Incorporate examples related to credit into math word problems.
- Incorporate examples related to individual credit in discussion of banks, government, and the recent recession.

*IEP goal:* The student will evaluate at least three colleges or universities for appropriate fit in regard to disability services in addition to standard selection criteria.

- Encourage or require this as a writing topic for a compare and contrast essay.

## Other Ways to Address Goals

Preparing students to make the transition out of school also involves simply increasing their awareness of the greater world. One way to do this is through service-learning activities, which wed community experiences to instruction and reflection (O'Connor, 2009). Carefully designed service-learning projects can connect academic goals and transition-related IEP goals together, allowing all students the opportunity to grow in their understanding of how they can affect the greater world. In addition, co-teachers can seek to make real-world connections in their daily instruction. See Box 11.4 for examples of ways to incorporate transition-related IEP goals into content-area instruction.

## ADOLESCENCE

A final consideration for co-teachers working in middle or high school settings is that their adolescent students will present challenges due to characteristics of their age group. Individuals during this time are experiencing a great deal of change in themselves and the way that the world interacts with them (Sabornie & deBettencourt, 2004). In school, they are dealing with increased academic responsibilities, increased social responsibilities (with little clarity about their new role in the social game), and increased responsibilities for their actions. During this time, typically developing students experience physical growth and growth in abilities to think in the abstract, to reflect, and to control information processing. Adolescents, especially those with disabilities, often appear very tough but can also be vulnerable and prone to emotional outbursts.

Students with disabilities may not make the physical and cognitive growth spurts that their peers without disabilities make. Co-teachers need

---

**BOX** | **11.5** | **Considerations for working with adolescents**

- Draw the line between teacher and friend. If you cross the line and become more friend than teacher, you lose authority and could end up in a sticky legal or ethical situation. When students forget that you are the authority, behavior problems may increase. Students may tell you personal things that you are obligated to report to administration or social services and then feel betrayed when you do report it. For co-teachers, specifically, if one co-teacher is seen as the "friend," it is likely that person will not be able to maintain an educational atmosphere when the other teacher is not present, and it is also likely that students will pit the co-teachers against each other because the students do not see the teachers as united.

- Be aware of who individual students are more comfortable communicating with. Do not require students with disabilities to go to the special education teacher with questions and vice versa. Be sensitive to potential personality conflicts with the students and work to avoid them.

- Avoid using sarcasm as humor. There will be at least one student in the class who will misread your tone and miss the sarcasm, especially if there are students with language-related disabilities in your class. If your co-teacher has said something you are not sure was received correctly, hop in to help set things straight: "Oh, Ms. Jones, you and your jokes!"

- Be sensitive to social issues that may be happening outside of the classroom, such as sporting, drama, and social events. Discuss with your co-teacher how you will handle these issues when they impede on your instructional time. Have a plan in place.

---

to be aware that educational differences will not go away in adolescence and in fact may grow deeper. In addition, co-teachers at the middle and secondary level need to be especially careful not to single out students for their differences. Though some adolescents will seek a unique label, most will not be excited to have personal information such as disability status, economic status, or religious status shared with the class, and such disclosures will cause trust issues. Research has demonstrated that the relationship between a teacher and a student can greatly affect socioemotional stability and related behaviors, including delinquency (Murray & Pianta, 2007). See Box 11.5 for considerations when working with adolescents.

## CONCLUSION

When reading through this chapter, the middle or high school teacher should have recognized many of the challenges he or she faces in a traditionally taught classroom. Many of the issues with planning instruction are the same in co-taught and traditionally taught classrooms, but the resources and approaches to instruction may change with a co-teacher by one's side. Co-teachers need to be a team, a united front working together to help all of the students in their class.

When reviewing the chapter checklist, can you check the items as complete? Can you recognize instructional strategies that support learning for all of your students in the co-taught middle or secondary classroom? Can you identify three strategies that can be used successfully in your classroom? Can you describe the unique needs of students in a co-taught class related to self-determination and self-advocacy? Can you create a co-teaching lesson plan that incorporates instructional strategies for all students, as well as accommodations and modifications for students with special needs?

 ## REFLECTIONS

- How will you accommodate your students who cannot comprehend the texts used in instruction?
- How will you work study skills into the classroom instruction?

 ## CONNECTIONS

All co-teachers

- Use the Co-Teaching Planning Checklist on page 68 and the accompanying DVD to plan your next lesson.
- How will you address self-determination or self-advocacy in the co-taught classroom?
- Plan to incorporate these skills into your next unit.

# Improve and Reflect on Relationships

# 12

# How Are We Doing?

---

**CHAPTER CHECKLIST**

Once you have read this chapter, you should be able to

- ○ Identify successful outcomes of co-teaching.
- ○ Set goals related to your co-taught classroom.
- ○ Evaluate your efficacy as a co-teacher.

---

 *WHAT'S ON THE DVD?*

Ed talks about formative assessment and making improvements in instruction from one year to the next.

Sherry and Craig talk about their reflection process and how they measure their success.

 *WHAT SHOULD I WATCH FOR ON THE DVD?*

- • What changes from one year to the next does Ed talk about?
- • How do Sherry and Craig determine if their co-teaching is successful?

In any new endeavor, people should seek perfection, or at least continuous improvement. In co-teaching, the two teachers involved should receive feedback in the form of formal and informal evaluations from their administrators (see Chapter 13), but they will find that engaging in self-reflection and self-assessment will provide them with feedback on a more continual basis and may be more meaningful for them as a pair. One advantage to co-teaching that teachers saw early in its inception is that teachers can "learn from one another through reflection" (Brody, 1994, p. 33). Though early benefits focused on teachers growing in their individual practice by working together, structured reflection will help co-teachers strengthen their joint practices and improve outcomes in their classroom.

Of course, when talking about assessment and outcomes, it is helpful to begin with a discussion about what the outcomes for co-teaching should be. Research is not very helpful on this front, as not much has been published related to how to measure or identify "good" co-teaching. To mimic the good lesson planning practice of starting with the outcome in mind, co-teachers need to think about and plan for outcomes of the co-teaching partnership from the beginning of the school year. Co-teachers should first identify what "success" will look like for their co-taught classroom, setting goals with those defined successes as outcomes, then determining how they will assess progress toward those goals and reach them.

## SETTING GOALS

Co-teachers can consult helpful resources when setting goals and choosing important outcomes for students. For instance, if setting an *instructional* goal, the teachers may begin by looking at the state academic standards. If setting a *behavioral* goal, the teachers will collect data to determine the student's current functional level and then set a goal based on reasonable improvement from the current level. In co-teaching there is no single set of published standards that is the ultimate definition of a "good" co-taught classroom, making it impossible to set goals using a template. Magiera and Simmons (2005) suggested looking for quality co-teaching in five categories: professionalism, classroom management, instructional process, learning groups, and student progress. Hang and Rabren (2009) suggested that the perspectives of the teachers and students and the academic and behavior performance of students provide good information about the efficacy of co-teaching.

Though all of these factors are important, researchers have concentrated on assessing co-teaching from an administrator's or researcher's point of view and not on how teachers can assess their own co-teaching. To assess the efficacy of co-teaching in their own classroom, admittedly more important than saying that co-teaching works in the abstract, teachers can isolate specific behaviors and take data on that behavior to set a goal (e.g., increasing the number of minutes per week they spend co-planning), and there is merit in that for some behaviors. However, teachers need to be cognizant of not getting caught up in assessing co-teaching behaviors and overlooking what we argue is the most important factor, which is the *impact on the student.*

## Student Outcomes

The question that guides decision making in schools should always be *What is best for the students?* As with any intervention or model, co-teaching needs to have a positive impact on students to justify continuing the model. Published literature on co-teaching has not demonstrated that the model has a singular, positive impact on student achievement (see Chapter 1), making it even more important that co-teachers pay attention to and specifically reflect on the outcomes for their students in the co-taught class.

There are two dimensions to the impact of co-teaching on students: academic (including IEP) and nonacademic. Students' academic achievement gives co-teachers a ready-made marker to assess their effectiveness as a team. Academic goals are identified for teachers by outside organizations, such as the state department of education and central office personnel or, for students with disabilities, an IEP team.

The nonacademic impact is more difficult to identify, though as co-teachers talk they can determine what they want their students to get from class besides academic knowledge. For starters, most co-teachers want the same comfort level for their students in the co-taught classroom as in their non-co-taught classroom, but the goal-setting should not stop at comparisons between the traditional and co-taught classes. Co-teachers may choose to consider student absence and tardy rates as indicators of student excitement about class. They may set goals related to how many students volunteer to respond in class or how student behavior reflects integration into one classroom, with students with disabilities seeking answers from the general education teacher and those without disabilities going to the special education teacher. They may also choose to set goals related to behavior management issues.

## Teacher Behaviors

Though student outcomes should be the number-one determining factor when looking at the efficacy of co-teachers, specific co-teaching behaviors have been noted as important for administrators to look for when they are observing co-taught classes (Gately, 2005; McDuffie, 2010; Rea & Connell, 2005a). Co-teachers should plan to assess themselves on the same behaviors that administrators will be looking for. Examples of teacher behaviors in specific lessons include both teachers taking an active role in instruction at some point in the class period, teachers communicating nonverbally, teachers appearing at ease and using humor, teachers incorporating evidenced-based methods, and teachers being familiar with the content and instructional methods involved in that lesson (Gately, 2005).

Equally important are behaviors that cannot be observed during a lesson. Teachers need to make use of co-planning time, need to plan for the needs of all of their students, and need to consider accommodations and modifications that may not make it into the final lesson. All of these things will be more difficult if the co-teachers are not working efficiently and contentedly together. Chapter 4 laid out some principles for communication and encouraged co-teachers to talk about how they will communicate. Some communication plans could be considered goals, such as how often the co-teachers will communicate. Co-teachers should consider the Co-Teacher's Oath on page 52 and the accompanying DVD when setting goals for their relationship. Harder to measure is contentment. It could be that co-teachers meet their goals related to how often and in what manner they will communicate, and that they meet their student outcome goals, but just do not enjoy working with each other. In those cases, we recommend that the co-teaching pair concentrate on maintaining high student achievement and consider asking for reassignment for the next school year.

## ASSESSING PROGRESS TOWARD GOALS

Setting goals is only effective if used as a part of a continuous improvement cycle (see Figure 12.1). Co-teachers need to set goals with data collection

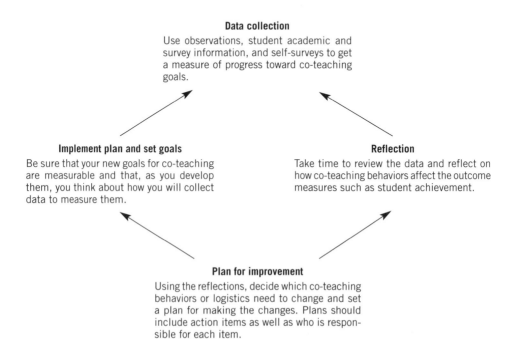

**Figure 12.1.** Continuous improvement cycle for co-teaching.

in mind. How will the co-teachers gather information to determine progress toward those goals? Think of self-assessment as progress monitoring for growth in co-teaching. Chapter 7 discussed formative assessment as it relates to student academic achievement, but the principles can be applied to any long-term goal. A weight-loss goal, for instance, is most effective if you take measures while working toward the goal instead of reaching the deadline to fit into the dress or suit and finding that your methods were not effective. In co-teaching it is even more important to continually assess and reflect on how things are going because two people are involved and they may have different opinions and perspectives on the efficacy of their co-teaching. Continuous assessment and reflection allows co-teachers an opportunity to share their points of view and resolve differences.

## Student Outcomes

Regularly measuring student academic performance and growth is a best practice regardless of whether students are in a co-taught classroom. Co-teachers should be using formative assessment for instructional decision making, and they can also use it as a tool to measure their effectiveness as a co-teaching team on the academic achievement or progress toward IEP goals of students in their co-taught class.

What are harder to measure are students' opinions related to the co-teaching dynamic in the classroom. Gerber and Popp (1999) used direct questions via student interviews to determine student perspectives on co-teaching. Questions ranged from what students liked and disliked about the co-taught classroom and having two teachers in the classroom to questions related to self-confidence and learning. Similarly, Hang and Rabren (2009) surveyed students with Likert scale (e.g., rating of 1–5) statements related to comparing their learning experiences, expectations and self-confidence, peer relationships, and academic efforts to those of a non-co-taught classroom. Co-teaching pairs could devise a simple survey for their students to gather similar data.

A nontraditional method for assessing the co-taught classroom involves drawings. Bessette's (2008) study used student drawings as a research tool and also provided teachers with an opportunity to reflect on many aspects of their co-taught classroom. Elementary and middle school students drew pictures to the prompt "Draw what it looks like in your classroom when both of your teachers are working" (2008, p. 1380) and provided descriptions of what they drew. Teachers viewed the drawings and reflected on what the drawing demonstrated to them about the student's perspective in the classroom. Some reflections were more strongly related to teacher behaviors, such as uneven or even role assignments between co-teachers, but other reflections drew information related to student outcomes, such as student understanding and classroom behaviors, from the drawings. Asking students to respond to a prompt such as this could provide a valuable

---

**BOX 12.1**    **Involving students in co-teaching assessment**

Elementary school
- Provide students with statements such as, "I feel happy asking both Mrs. Jones and Mr. Smith questions." Have them circle a smiley face or a sad face to indicate agreement or disagreement.
- Ask students to write about a day in their classroom.

Middle and high school
- Provide students with statements such as, "I get more attention in my co-taught classes than my non–co-taught classes." Have them respond on a Likert scale of *agree*, *neutral or don't know*, or *disagree*.
- Ask students to reflect on how their co-taught class is different from their other classes.

---

springboard for co-teacher reflection and self-assessment. Teachers have to know their students, though, and may want to use a more structured format, such as a Likert scale, to limit the amount of time the assessment takes from instruction or to better control the focus of the data they receive. See Box 12.1 for some examples of how to involve students in co-teaching assessment in elementary, middle, and high schools.

### Teacher Behaviors

Conversations and reflections are the greatest tool for self-assessment of teacher behaviors. The quality of assessment will depend greatly on what the teachers use as a springboard for the reflection and on their willingness to communicate honestly and openly. Drawings or student surveys are one way to gather information related to teacher behaviors from the student perspective. Using a checklist of co-teaching goals and behaviors, either one that the co-teachers have developed together or the Co-Teaching Self-Assessment on page 163 and also on the accompanying DVD, is another place to begin reflection. It may be helpful for each co-teacher to reflect independently and then share the assessments with his or her counterpart.

Another tool for the reflective process is video of the co-taught classroom. When an administrator observes the pair, he or she will be able to take data in real time, counting the number of student responses and the number of times that the co-teachers switch lead roles. However, teachers are not easily able to keep track of their behaviors as they are teaching. By occasionally videotaping the co-taught lesson, teachers can reflect on their actions, noting what works well and what does not work well, and use that as a springboard for conversation. See Box 12.2 for examples of questions co-teachers should ask as they reflect on their teaching in individual lessons.

# Co-Teaching Self-Assessment

| | | |
|---|---|---|
| I feel like an equal partner with my co-teacher. | Yes | No |
| I feel respected by my co-teacher. | Yes | No |
| When my co-teacher and I talk about the classroom, I feel like my opinion matters. | Yes | No |
| I am comfortable with the level of personal relationship I have with my co-teacher. | Yes | No |
| When my co-teacher and I talk about the classroom, we make decisions with the needs of the students coming before our own preferences. | Yes | No |
| When my co-teacher and I disagree, I am comfortable with how we resolve the difference. | Yes | No |
| My co-teacher and I make time to plan together. | Yes | No |

How often?

| | | |
|---|---|---|
| When planning instruction, we consider the items on the Co-Teaching Planning Checklist (Chapter 6). | Yes | No |

My co-teacher and I share responsibilities in

| | | |
|---|---|---|
| Planning | Yes | No |
| Ensuring that we think about all students as individuals when planning | Yes | No |
| Grading | Yes | No |
| Contacting parents | Yes | No |
| Making copies, posting to the online platform (e.g., Blackboard, E-School), other administrative duties | Yes | No |
| Enforcing behavioral expectations (not chewing gum, raising one's hand to speak) | Yes | No |
| Enforcing academic expectations (homework, studying) | Yes | No |
| Taking concerns to the administration | Yes | No |

---

**BOX** **12.2** **Questions for reflection on a lesson**

- How prepared were we going into this lesson? (Ask this so that you can see the correlation between planning practices and lesson outcomes.)
- What worked well? What did not work well?
- How engaged were the students? Was there a difference in engagement for students with and without disabilities?
- Did we have to deal with certain student behaviors? Did we take care of the behavior in a way that both of us is comfortable with? Do we need to rethink what to do if we have behavior issues in the future?
- What were the accommodations and modifications we planned to meet individual students' needs? Did they align with those needs? Did we implement them seamlessly so that students were not singled out?
- Did the methods we used for instruction meet the students' needs and align with the content?
- Did we both take the lead role at different points in the lesson? Were we both comfortable with the roles we took? Do we need to adjust how we divide the leader role in the future?
- Did we both feel like equal partners in this lesson? In the classroom as a whole?
- Did we need to deviate from our original plan? If so, were we able to do so smoothly? How did we communicate it? Is there a way to do this better in the future?
- Did we present a united front? Did students get the same answers about policies, procedures, and methods from both of us?
- Does postlesson assessment demonstrate student understanding? If not, how will we adjust future lessons?

## CONCLUSION

The importance of self-assessment and reflection cannot be underplayed. Teachers can only strive to improve if they can identify how they are doing right now. Can you identify variables that can speak to your effectiveness as a co-teacher? Can you set goals for yourself in your co-taught classroom? How will you determine you have reached those goals?

 ***REFLECTIONS***

- Go through the Co-Teaching Self-Assessment on page 163 and on the accompanying DVD, using the prompts as a springboard for reflection.

**CONNECTIONS**

Experienced co-teachers

- What areas do you see that need improvement?
- Videotape one of your co-taught lessons and use Box 12.2 to reflect on your teaching. With your co-teacher, set goals for improvement and decide how you will track progress toward those goals.

Beginning co-teachers

- Videotape one of your co-taught lessons and use Box 12.2 to reflect on your teaching. With your co-teacher, set goals for improvement and decide how you will track progress toward those goals.

Prospective co-teachers

- Review your responses to Reflections and Connections sections in prior chapters. How has this process of reflection affected your views on or the quality of your co-teaching?

# 13

# Working with Others in the School

---

## CHAPTER CHECKLIST

Once you have read this chapter, you should be able to

○ Identify ways in which co-teachers may interact with administrators.
○ Identify nontraditional co-teaching pairs.
○ Identify considerations when working with an instructional assistant (IA) in a co-taught classroom.

---

 ### WHAT'S ON THE DVD?

Debbie, an administrator, talks about a master schedule that supports co-teaching and offers advice to administrators at schools with co-teaching.

Debbie talks about how she, as an administrator, mediates co-teachers who are not getting along.

Tom, a special educator whose identity is protected in the DVD because he has not had good co-teaching experiences, talks about how he and his co-teacher with whom he does not have a good working relationship make it work.

**WHAT SHOULD I WATCH FOR ON THE DVD?**

- Does your administrator share the same philosophy as Debbie?
- What tactics does Tom use to make his co-teaching situation as successful as possible?

The time is past when teachers could close their classroom doors and separate what they do in their classroom from the rest of the school's workings. Classrooms are no longer isolated islands. Today's schools are places where many different individuals come into each classroom and where teachers share instructional ideas and feedback. In such classrooms, there may be two teachers instructing, a school counselor observing, and parents volunteering. Administrators are in and out for observations and may encourage or require classroom teachers to observe each other to promote breaking down divisions and moving away from the old idea that teachers' ideas and materials are their sacred property. Schools are places of collaboration, with many schools following models of professional learning communities to encourage an open flow of ideas between teachers, aimed at improving instructional practices across the school as a whole (Jacobson, 2010). Co-teaching teams, like all teachers, will find that they cannot exist by working solely within their classroom but must also work with other people in the school to be most successful. Administrator interactions may be the most common for some co-teaching pairs, but co-teachers will also work with other teachers, IAs and paraprofessionals, and related services personnel such as speech-language pathologists (SLPs) and occupational therapists.

## ADMINISTRATORS

As discussed in Chapter 5, administrator support is vital to successful co-teaching. Administrators hold the strings that can fix many of the common problems with co-teaching implementation, such as co-planning time, student's scheduling, and staff development (Walther-Thomas, 1997). Administrators are also helpful problem solvers and referees when co-teachers have disagreements or face issues in their classroom that they have difficulty resolving.

In addition, co-teachers need to be aware that some of the support items we have talked about as being controlled by administration may not be directly handled by the principal or assistant principal. In middle and high schools, guidance counselors are often heavily involved with, or solely responsible for, the master schedule. In these situations, involving the guidance counselor in discussions about how the co-teachers envision the class, in terms of student make-up, is helpful (Gerber & Popp, 2000). It may be

| | General education science teacher | Special education teacher | General education English teacher |
|---|---|---|---|
| *Period 1* | *Planning* | *Planning* | *Planning* |
| Period 2 | Co-taught earth science | | English 10 |
| Period 3 | Earth science | Self-contained English 10 | Lunch duty |
| Period 4 | Lunch duty | Basic skills | English 10 |
| Period 5 | Earth science | Lunch duty | English 10 |
| Period 6 | Earth science | Co-taught English 10 | |
| Period 7 | Co-taught earth science | | English 10 |

**Figure 13.1.**   Sample middle or high school schedule. (*Note*: The special education teacher has the same planning period as both of his or her co-teachers, allowing him or her to meet with each co-teacher during scheduled planning time, though probably not in every planning period.)

wise for co-teachers to sit down with guidance counselors, or whoever handles schedules, to select specific students for the classes. See Figures 13.1 and 13.2 for sample schedules that support co-teaching.

Administrators and principals have multiple responsibilities in schools. In elementary schools, principals function as disciplinarians with students, complaint officers for parents, and school leaders (Green, 2008). As school leaders, principals also coordinate schoolwide programs; provide the "vision" of the school culture; and provide support for teachers, parents, and students to achieve success. In middle and high schools, the principal spends more time on administrative functions; however, he or she remains the school leader. The administrator roles related to co-teaching can be summarized as *school leader, matchmaker,* and *referee.*

## School Leader

The administrator or principal has responsibility for the school climate or environment. For example, some administrators reward or recognize achievements in co-teaching and ensure that adequate co-planning time is available (Hines, 2008). This helps to create an environment where teachers feel comfortable co-teaching. However, other schools are less friendly to co-teaching. For example, co-teaching pairs are initiated by the teachers themselves without any support from the principal, or co-teaching pairs

Figure 13.2 — Sample elementary school schedule (two schedule tables)

**Schedule 1**

|   | Kindergarten | Primary language arts lab A.M. | Upper math lab A.M. | Primary math lab P.M. | Upper language arts lab P.M. |
|---|---|---|---|---|---|
| K | Teacher A |  |  |  |  |
| 1 |  | Teacher B |  | Teacher D |  |
| 2 |  |  | Teacher C |  |  |
| 3 |  |  |  |  |  |
| 4 |  |  |  |  | Teacher E |
| 5 |  |  |  |  |  |
| 6 |  |  |  |  |  |

**Schedule 2**

|   | Primary language arts inclusion A.M. | Primary language arts inclusion A.M. | Upper math 4 inclusion A.M. | Upper math 5 inclusion A.M. | Upper math 6 inclusion A.M. |   | Primary math inclusion P.M. | Primary math inclusion P.M. | Upper language arts inclusion P.M. | Upper language arts inclusion P.M. | Upper language arts inclusion P.M. |
|---|---|---|---|---|---|---|---|---|---|---|---|
| K | Teacher F |  |  |  |  | K | Teacher F |  |  |  |  |
| 1 |  | Teacher G |  |  |  | 1 |  |  |  |  |  |
| 2 |  |  |  |  |  | 2 |  | Teacher G |  |  |  |
| 3 |  |  |  |  |  | 3 |  |  |  |  |  |
| 4 |  |  | Teacher H |  |  | 4 |  |  | Teacher H |  |  |
| 5 |  |  |  | Teacher C |  | 5 |  |  |  | Teacher H |  |
| 6 |  |  |  |  | Teacher E | 6 |  |  |  |  | Teacher B |

**Figure 13.2.** Sample elementary school schedule. (Reprinted by permission from Debbie Diaz-Arnold.)

are initiated by the principal but without training opportunities or adequate co-planning time provided.

Co-teachers will quickly identify the type of school environment in which they are teaching. Ideally, all co-teachers would be assigned to teach in schools that support co-teaching; however, this is not the reality. When teaching in a less-than-friendly co-teaching environment, co-teachers need to focus on being positive. Remember, the principal is your boss, and no boss wants to be bombarded with complaints and negative attitudes. Co-teachers can agree to try the following suggestions to help create a more positive co-teaching atmosphere:

1.  Invite administrators into your classroom to see co-teaching.
2.  Share articles on co-teaching with others in your school.
3.  Share classroom success stories with others, including your principal.
4.  Be positive in your interactions with the administrators. Generally, you should try to maintain positive interactions with everyone in the school, but to elicit administrator support it is vital that you are respectfully enthusiastic.

## Matchmaker

The principal or special education administrator may be responsible for pairing co-teachers because they are often responsible for teaching assignments. In some schools, administrators are focused on increasing the number of co-taught classrooms. In these situations, it may be most helpful to identify potential co-teaching partners and make suggestions to the administrators before you are assigned to teach with someone else. Often, co-teaching assignments are made with consideration of the school's master schedule rather than pairing teachers who may work well together. Please see Chapter 3 for suggestions on identifying a potential co-teaching partner.

Another "matchmaking" issue is that administrators may change teaching assignments year to year. This may be due to administrative factors such as number of students enrolled, achievement scores for specific subject areas, and personnel considerations. As it takes time to create a successful co-teaching team, this year-to-year change in partners does not promote success. Remember, co-teaching requires flexibility and a willingness to adapt. Should your co-teaching team be separated, try to remain positive and build a new relationship with your assigned co-teacher. Chapter 5 provides some suggestions if you are happily co-teaching and want to remain co-teaching with your current partner.

## Referee

As previously mentioned, the administrator or principal can assist co-teaching teams with problem solving. Co-teachers can approach administrators individually to talk through and get advice about a concern with a co-teacher, but much like marriage counseling it will be more effective if both members of the team go to the administrator together. However, administrators should not be called in for every little disagreement. Co-teachers need to try to resolve the conflict themselves before going to the administration (see more on conflict resolution in Chapter 4).

Sometimes the conflict between co-teachers is irresolvable and a continuation of the team is not possible. The co-teachers may believe that dissolution of their partnership is inevitable and the only way to set aside the conflict. This is a serious situation that can be likened to a divorce and should not be undertaken without thoughtful consideration. Both co-teachers will need to communicate with their principal or administrator to help resolve this situation. See Box 13.1 for suggestions on dissolving a co-teaching team.

---

**BOX 13.1    Dissolving a co-teaching team**

A failed partnership can elicit feelings of inadequacy, frustration, anger, or even resentment. Although these feelings are very human, they do not assist in resolving the conflict or differences that caused the partnership to fail. During a divorce, parents are often counseled to put the needs of their children first; co-teachers are similarly reminded to put the needs of their students first. The following are suggestions for co-teachers who are dissolving their team:

1. Share responsibility for the failure. Do not blame the other teacher or yourself.

2. Be professional in your interactions with each other. This can be a very tense situation and you may feel emotional. Try to maintain your composure and be polite with each other.

3. Maintain your instructional focus. Your students need you to guide them through the content they must learn. You and your co-teacher need to ensure that your instruction supports student success.

4. Recognize that you and your co-teacher will likely continue teaching at the same school. Do not try to gain support from other teachers by discussing your co-teacher problems or issues. Do not engage in teacher lounge gossip about your co-teacher.

5. Create a plan or agreement on how you will continue teaching together until the partnership is dissolved. Often, it is not possible to change co-teaching assignments before the end of the school year; therefore, the co-teachers need to agree on how they will interact with each other until they are no longer partners.

6. Reflect on your co-teaching. What did you learn that might benefit your future co-teaching relationships? How will you work better with your next co-teacher?

## OTHER TEACHERS AND RELATED SERVICES PERSONNEL

Though we have talked about co-teachers as being a special educator and a general educator, co-teaching can take place between a general or special educator and a teacher of "specials" or electives, such as music, library, home economics, or computer, or also between a licensed teacher and a licensed related services professional, such as an SLP or occupational therapist. Very little research has been done related to the efficacy or prevalence of classrooms in which a special education or general education teacher co-teaches with another professional. One study found a decrease in referrals for speech services when a special education teacher and SLP co-taught with a general education teacher in a first-grade classroom for 8 hours a week (Reblin, 1994). Another set of authors described a co-teaching partnership between a second-grade general education teacher and a literacy support specialist, but took no measureable outcomes and only concluded that students were engaged and learned the content (Paugh, Carey, King-Jackson, & Russell, 2007). Porter (2009) described a partnership between a literacy coach and an English language learner teacher as they taught students whose first language was not English to read, comprehend, and appreciate Shakespeare, but again the author did not take data on student engagement or achievement.

This literature related to nontraditional co-teaching pairs mimics articles already discussed related to traditional pairings; there are no strong data indicating whether co-teaching affects student achievement. The same principles discussed throughout this book can be applied to these nontraditional co-teaching pairs, such as focusing on communication, being positive, and collecting data (Collett, 2008). Teachers may seek a co-teaching relationship with a nontraditional partner because of 1) a lack of skill development expertise, for instance, the example of the SLP and general education teacher (Reblin, 1994) in which the SLP brought additional language development experiences and activities; 2) overlapping content or interdisciplinary projects, such as an English teacher partnering with the social studies teacher for a joint unit on civics and speech writing; or 3) a desire to share expertise and experiences.

Even traditional co-teaching pairs will find it helpful to work with other teachers and related services personnel in the school. For instance, participating in grade-level or contentwide curriculum planning is equally beneficial for a co-teaching team as for individual teachers. Co-teachers who have students with disabilities in their classroom may find that they often have additional adults in their classroom because of students receiving services such as speech or occupational therapy. Though these professionals may be providing minimal services, the co-teaching team needs to work collaboratively with them to ensure that the students benefit from their limited time together. Box 13.2 offers discussion points for related services personnel who work within your co-taught classroom.

---

**BOX** **13.2** **Discussion points for working with related services professionals**

- On what goals are the student(s) receiving services working?
- Is there something you need to see the student engaged in while you are in the class?
- How regular will your visits be? If irregular, how far in advance will we know you are coming and how will you notify us?
- When you are working with the student(s), should we avoid giving him or her additional prompts and direction?
- Can we schedule a time or method for feedback and reflection on the students' progress?
- Will you need to pull the student out of the classroom to work with him or her? If so, will this occur every time you visit, or just sometimes? Do we need to make sure you have somewhere to go?
- If you will work with the student in the room during regular instruction, what kind of room and space do you need?
- What should we tell the other students about why you are in the classroom?

---

## INSTRUCTIONAL ASSISTANTS

Not all co-taught classrooms will have IAs in the classroom. They are more common when the number of students with disabilities is proportionally higher than average, when a specific student has intense needs and requires a one-to-one assistant, and in elementary schools where it may be standard practice to have IA support in classrooms. If an IA will be in the room during instructional time, co-teachers need to have a plan for how to use the IA, how to communicate duties to the IA, and how to address any issues or concerns that come up related to the IA (Rea & Connell, 2005b). Teachers are not trained to be supervisors and managers for other adults, and the fact that two teachers hold the supervisory role in a co-taught classroom could further complicate matters. Co-teachers who will be working with an IA in the classroom should consider, together, the questions in Box 13.3 to make best use of the additional adult in the classroom.

It is also possible that an IA will serve in the role of co-teacher, in the room to serve the educational needs of the students with disabilities but doing more than providing one-to-one assistance. It is imperative to remember that IAs, as a general rule, do not have an education background and training and are *not* to be at the instructional helm of the classroom. The supervising teacher needs to provide guidance and set expectations for IAs, even those with a great deal of experience. It may be that the classroom teacher and the IA become comfortable enough with each other that the IA leads homework review with the large group, for instance, providing

---

**BOX** **13.3** **Considerations for co-teaching with instructional assistant (IA) support**

- Who will be the IA's point person for feedback and questions?
- When and how will we communicate daily lesson responsibilities to the IA?
- How will we share appropriate information about the students with the IA?
- Who will talk with the IA about confidentiality and our approach for honoring individual student confidentiality in our classroom?
- How can we best use the IA in the classroom to support our instructional goals and the needs of the students?
- How can the IA help with data collection? Who will train the IA in data collection tools and methods?
- Who will train, model, and communicate our behavior management and instructional techniques?
- Respecting that the IA has perspectives to share with us, how will we encourage the IA to be a member of our collaborative classroom community?

  In addition, keep in mind the following when working with an IA:

- Find some time in the day to plan with the IA, but remember that IA contract times are different from those of teachers and that IAs are sometimes strictly held to their contract times.
- Remember that *you* are the instructional leader. Ultimately, the teacher is responsible for student safety and learning. Though it may be appropriate for IAs to take instructional roles at times, it is only with strong teacher direction and guidance.

  *Sources:* Devlin (2008); Wadsworth & Knight (1996).

---

the teacher with the opportunity to work more intensely with a few students, or that the two engage in Station Teaching, with the teacher providing heavy direction to the IA for instructional strategies and methods. See Box 13.3 for considerations for the supervising teacher when the IA takes on the co-teaching role.

## CONCLUSION

Co-teachers cannot exist simply as two teachers working in one classroom. They must work with administration to receive support, and they must work with other resources and adults in the school who may have expertise to share or reason to enter the classroom. Co-teachers need to think about their relationship with others in the school and be ready to approach those relationships, especially with administrators and others who will come into their shared classroom, as a team.

**REFLECTIONS**

- What roles do you see others—such as administrators, related services personnel, and IAs—playing in your co-teaching relationship?

 **CONNECTIONS**

Experienced and beginning co-teachers

- Have you had any conflicts with your co-teacher that you think need mediation by an outside party? How will you approach it with your administrator and co-teacher?
- If you work with an IA in the classroom, how do you, your co-teacher, and the IA balance and play off of each other? Do you and your co-teacher take the strong instructional lead? What is your combined management style, and is it working?

Prospective co-teachers

- Besides a general education or special education teacher, who else would it be appropriate for you to co-teach with, even just for a specific unit or content?

# 14

# Working with Parents

## CHAPTER CHECKLIST

Once you have read this chapter, you should be able to

○ Describe how you and your co-teacher will consistently and regularly communicate with parents.

○ Create a plan for holding joint parent conferences.

○ Identify the responsibilities for both the general education teacher and the special education teacher in IEP meetings.

○ Describe how you and your co-teacher will incorporate sensitive communication approaches for families with diverse needs.

## *WHAT'S ON THE DVD?*

Craig and Sherry talk about how they communicate with parents.

## *WHAT SHOULD I WATCH FOR ON THE DVD?*

• This method made the most sense for this co-teaching pair. What makes sense for you?

Every teacher is responsible for communicating with parents, although the special education teacher often has more contact and specific responsibilities, as outlined in IDEA 2004. Just as co-teachers are encouraged to view the students as "our students," they should also consider the parents as "our parents." Most teachers recognize the importance of good communication between school and home to support student success (Friend & Cook, 2007). However, in a co-taught classroom, both teachers must agree on how frequently the communication should occur, how the communication will occur, and how both teachers will respond when there are difficulties.

Co-teachers will also communicate with parents at parent conferences and IEP meetings. Again, both teachers need to identify how they will interact together in these situations. For example, will both teachers be present at a parent conference? If so, how can they ensure that the parent is comfortable with both of them? Often, special education teachers are also case managers for individual students and have responsibility for coordinating IEP meetings, so the special education teacher may have more contact with parents of students receiving special education services. How will both teachers be involved with these parents?

## COMMUNICATING WITH PARENTS

IDEA 2004 mandates that parents should be consistently and regularly informed about their child's progress on IEP goals, and special education teachers are aware of this requirement. This communication can be in the form of weekly progress notes sent home or quarterly grade reports. Although there is no corresponding legislation that outlines the responsibilities of communicating with parents of general education students, they should also have regular communication with their child's teachers, perhaps through an e-mail or a newsletter that provides information about what is happening in the class or, often, through quarterly grade reports and parent conferences (Gorman, 2004).

In previous chapters, co-teachers have been encouraged to establish trust, respect, and communication with each other. The same principles apply to building parent relationships with both co-teachers. Once a co-teaching team has partnered, it needs to decide how often it will communicate with parents. Consider some of the following suggestions for communicating general classroom information.

- Daily notes in the backpack might be appropriate for some students with disabilities but are generally not appropriate for every student in the classroom.
- Weekly progress notes might be appropriate for all students in the class.
- Monthly newsletters with classroom highlights might be used.
- Daily or weekly electronic posting of homework and class announcements are helpful communications (e.g., BlackBoard software).

- E-mail updates may also be used; check school policies.
- Quarterly and interim grade reports might be sent home as progress measures for all students.

Both teachers should consider who will be responsible for sending home these progress notes and newsletters. Again, both teachers' names should appear on all notes.

At the start of the school year, teachers often send home a letter to parents. In many situations, this is the first contact with the parents. These letters can be helpful in providing an introduction to class expectations, explaining teacher preferences, and providing teacher contact information. See Box 14.1 for suggestions for an introductory letter to parents and Figure 14.1 for an example.

Often, the introductory letter is also an invitation for the parents to attend Back-to-School Night. Elementary co-teachers should review the suggestions in Chapter 10 for Back-to-School Night. Middle and high school co-teachers are reminded that Back-to-School Night at their schools is important, though fewer parents may attend. It is helpful for both teachers to preplan how they will communicate their partnership to parents (e.g., both names on handouts, both names on the door, both teachers greeting and talking to all parents).

Co-teachers should consider when they will call parents at home regarding an individual student. They also need to consider who will make the telephone call. Will the special education teacher only call parents of students with disabilities? Will the teachers alternate calling (and if so, how will they make sure that one of them is not only calling about problems while the other one is only calling about good news)? Often, parents are only contacted by telephone when there is a problem or behavior issue with their student (Gorman, 2004). When parents are telephoned only

---

**BOX 14.1 Suggestions for start-of-school letter**

- Be friendly
- Begin with a positive statement (e.g., "We are excited to meet your child").
- Provide contact information for both teachers (e-mail, telephone).
- Decide if parents can telephone you at home or on your cell phone.
- If parents can telephone you at home, specify when they can call (e.g., not on weekends, before 8 P.M.).
- Convey any important information that parents need to know (Back-to-School Night date, what information will be posted online and when).
- End with a positive statement (e.g., "We are looking forward to meeting you").

*Note:* Please make sure to use the first-person plural forms "we" and "our." Both teachers' names and contact information should be on the letter.

Dear Parents,

We are the teachers for your child's [insert grade or subject] class. We are looking forward to getting to know your child and meeting with you. Please feel free to contact either of us when you have questions about your child's performance or just want to check in. Our e-mail addresses and our school voicemail numbers are provided below.

The school's Open House [or Back-to-School Night] is scheduled for [insert date and time]. We look forward to meeting you and hearing about your child. Please bring with you a short note telling us about your son or daughter. We'd like to know about his or her strengths, areas you feel he or she needs help on, and how you think he or she learns best. We look forward to meeting you. Thank you.

Special education teacher          General education teacher
[School]                          [School]
[School telephone/e-mail]         [School telephone/e-mail]

**Figure 14.1.** Sample introductory start-of-school letter. (*Note:* You may want to provide teacher names without noting which teacher is the special education or general education teacher.) (DEBETTENCOURT, LAURIE U.; HOWARD, LORI, A., EFFECTIVE SPECIAL EDUCATION TEACHER: PRACTICAL GUIDE FOR SUCCESS, THE, 1st Edition, © 2007. p. 34. Reprinted by permission of Pearson Education, Inc., Upper Saddle River, NJ.)

when there is a problem, they may begin to dread or fear hearing from the teacher. This can create a barrier to communication, so we encourage co-teachers to also call parents when they have positive behaviors or incidents to report to parents.

## CONDUCTING PARENT CONFERENCES AND INDIVIDUALIZED EDUCATION PROGRAM MEETINGS

Notes, e-mails, or telephone calls provide easy methods of communication; however, there are times when parents and co-teachers need to meet face to face. There are several types of parent–co-teacher interactions, including 1) informal, unscheduled meetings, 2) formal parent–teacher conferences, and 3) IEP meetings.

### Informal or Unscheduled Parent–Teacher Meetings

Informal meetings can occur in a variety of ways: A parent brings a child to school and asks if he or she can chat with you. A parent comes to your classroom after school and wants to talk. You are heading to the copy room near the office and a parent stops you with a question. Although such meetings may be more common at the elementary level, they can happen to any teacher.

How you and your co-teacher respond will depend on the nature of the parent's concern. For example, is the parent angry regarding a classroom assignment? Or, is the parent concerned because the student's grandparent has been diagnosed with a serious illness? You or your co-teacher need to determine the purpose of the informal meeting. Is it to convey information? Is it to "lobby" for the child? The purpose may dictate whether the co-teacher who was approached talks to the parent alone or whether he or she suggests setting up a formal meeting or finding the co-teacher and meeting at that moment.

Sometimes, the parent needs basic information and there is no need for both teachers to talk to the parent, but often there may be a need to schedule a formal meeting so that the concerns can be adequately addressed (deBettencourt & Howard, 2007). In the latter case, reassure the parent that you recognize his or her concern and would like to schedule a meeting with the parent and the co-teaching team. This meeting should be scheduled within a short time frame. Perhaps you need to ask the parent to return for a parent conference at the end of the day. Whenever possible, both teachers should be present at this meeting.

## Formal Parent–Teacher Conferences

These are often the primary face-to-face interaction between parents and teachers. Co-teachers need to address how they will conduct these joint conferences before scheduling them. This is another area to discuss once a co-teaching partnership has been created.

Parent–teacher conferences should follow a three-step process to ensure success: preconference planning, the conference, and postconference follow-up. Co-teachers should discuss who will take responsibility for each step.

1. *Preplanning stage*—Which co-teacher will schedule the meeting? Which co-teacher will be responsible for identifying agenda items and collecting samples of the student's work or behavior? If a room needs to be reserved, who will do this?
2. *Conference stage*—Which co-teacher will start the meeting? Does one co-teacher know the parent better and therefore should greet the parent? Who will do the introductions? Who will manage the agenda?
3. *Postconference stage*—Which co-teacher will follow up with the parent? Which co-teacher will be responsible for implementing any changes regarding the student or communication with the parent? If another meeting is to be scheduled, which teacher will be responsible?

## Individualized Education Program Meetings

Co-teachers will need to recognize that the special education teacher has specific responsibilities in an IEP meeting. Often, the special education teacher is also the student's case manager and conducts the IEP meeting. In addition, there are guidelines and timeframes for meetings that the special education teacher must follow. IDEA 2004 requires that a general education teacher also be in the meeting to provide input on the general education curriculum.

IEP meetings also should follow the three-step conference process. During the preplanning stage, teachers should solicit parental input on IEP goals and objectives. During the IEP meeting, parents should be asked for their input and ideas regarding the student's performance and future goals. IEP meetings may be emotionally difficult for parents, and teachers are reminded to be sensitive to parental feelings (Gorman, 2004). Often, the school members of an IEP team want to resolve any IEP issues quickly, whereas parents want to more fully discuss their concerns. Please remember to carefully listen to parents' concerns. After all, it is their child being discussed. Finally, once the meeting is concluded, there should be follow up with the parents to ensure that any concerns were addressed and that the parents are satisfied with the IEP. Again, the co-teachers should strive to provide a unified team during these meetings. Both co-teachers should be available to the parents as needed.

## WORKING TO RESOLVE DIFFERENCES

Sometimes a parent may feel more affinity for one of the co-teachers. Due to the responsibilities of case management and IEP meetings, special education teachers often have more contact with parents and thus the opportunity to build a stronger relationship. This situation can be very helpful for both co-teachers, but there can be difficulties, too.

Parents may want to complain or vent about the general education co-teacher to the special education teacher (Gorman, 2004). This is a very difficult situation, and the teacher must maintain professionalism. The teacher in this situation is advised to be empathetic and listen to the parent while not engaging in negative comments or "trash talk" about the co-teacher. Should this type of situation escalate or continue, co-teachers should seek administrator help. Administrators have experience and training to help diffuse difficult situations with parents (Gorman, 2004).

When there are difficulties with parents, it is important that co-teachers document all communication. Special education teachers are required to maintain documentation of parental contacts for the students on their caseload, not just when there is a conflict or difficulty, and we recommend this as standard practice for students without disabilities, too. Both co-teachers need to plan how they will note and maintain this documentation. For example, will each teacher create a parent contact log (a document that notes communication via telephone call, e-mail, or meetings) or will each teacher make notes on the same document? Due to the Family Educational Rights and Privacy Act (FERPA) of 1974 (PL 93-380), for confidentiality reasons the documentation (or log) should be individualized and not contain contacts for more than one student (U.S. Department of Education, 2010). Please see Figure 14.2 for an example of a Parent Contact Log that can be used to document communication with parents.

Both co-teachers need to recognize that parents of students with disabilities have specific legal rights designated through IDEA 2004. IDEA provides parents with the right to request a due process hearing if they disagree with the IEP team or items on the IEP. Due process hearings can be lengthy, time-consuming, and contentious; therefore, it is often in the best

# Parent Contact Log

Student name _____          Telephone (H) _____

Parents' names _____          Telephone (W) _____

Address _____          Telephone (W) _____

E-mail _____

Student schedule

| Time/block | Subject | Teacher/room |
|---|---|---|
|  |  |  |
|  |  |  |
|  |  |  |
|  |  |  |
|  |  |  |
|  |  |  |

Parent/guardian contact log

| Date | Who initiated contact? | How was contact initiated? (phone, note, or conference) | Reason | Follow up | Resolution | Co-teacher notified/ discussed (initial and date) |
|---|---|---|---|---|---|---|
|  |  |  |  |  |  |  |
|  |  |  |  |  |  |  |
|  |  |  |  |  |  |  |
|  |  |  |  |  |  |  |
|  |  |  |  |  |  |  |
|  |  |  |  |  |  |  |

**Figure 14.2.**   Parent Contact Log. (DEBETTENCOURT, LAURIE U.; HOWARD, LORI, A., EFFECTIVE SPECIAL EDUCA-TION TEACHER: PRACTICAL GUIDE FOR SUCCESS, THE, 1st Edition, © 2007. p. 35. Reprinted by permission of Pearson Education, Inc., Upper Saddle River, NJ.)

interest of both the IEP team and the student to resolve parental concerns in a timely and sensitive manner. Although the special education teacher has responsibilities delineated through legislation, it is important that both co-teachers recognize the importance of resolving difficulties with the parent.

## WORKING WITH ALL OF OUR PARENTS

In 2004, the poverty rate for children younger than the age of 18 was 17.8%, representing 13 million children (Denavas-Walt, Proctor, & Lee, 2005). Parents may be too stressed to help a child with homework as they are trying to ensure that the family has food or shelter. Parents may not be able to take time off from their jobs to attend a parent conference or IEP meeting. These situations are sometimes interpreted as the fault of an uncaring parent; however, the parent may have competing priorities that co-teachers are unaware of. Co-teachers should recognize that families and students have lives outside of school. Given the devastating effects of poverty, co-teachers should be sensitive and may want to know the community resources available to help families (deBettencourt & Howard, 2007). Often, the school has a social worker or guidance counselor who is equipped to assist these families.

There has also been a rising trend toward nontraditional families including grandparents as primary caregivers for their grandchildren, same-sex parents, divorced parents, homeless families, and/or foster parents (Gorman, 2004). Each of these situations involves unique challenges and opportunities for communication. Co-teachers should strive to be sensitive to all of these families, and one of the advantages of co-teaching is that two teachers can work together to find solutions for all of the students.

Schools are also becoming more ethnically diverse, and this diversity may present challenges to co-teachers (Johnson, 2003). Many co-taught classrooms include students who come from other countries or cultures. These students may be known as English speakers of other languages or English language learners. These students can have a disability, too. Many of the students (and their parents) may be learning the English language, so communication may be a barrier for them (deBettencourt & Howard, 2007). Parents may not have the language skills to fully participate in a conference or IEP meeting. They may not understand notes that are sent home. Co-teachers should work together to ensure that parents can participate in their student's education by coordinating conferences and communication and discussing appropriate resources. Co-teachers are reminded that many school districts have translation services and other resources, which may be required to be provided for some situations such as IEP meetings. Know what resources are available!

In addition to language issues, co-teachers should be aware of and sensitive to cultural issues (deBettencourt & Howard, 2007). It is impossible to detail all cultural taboos, preferences, and differences in any one book;

however, many school districts have resources to assist teachers with common local concerns.

There are some unique cultural challenges that can occur in the co-taught classroom. For example, what if the co-teaching team consists of a male and female teacher? In some cultures, the man will be seen as the leader, and parents may only want to communicate with him. This may cause some discomfort for the female teacher. The female teacher may want to "confront" this issue with the family; however, this may not be the most appropriate action. Both teachers should carefully consider how best to work with the student. Alienating a family from a different culture is not in the student's best interest. Ultimately, the two teachers must find a way to work with the family. The male teacher may need to take the lead for issues with this particular student.

There are often issues related to age. For example, what if a younger teacher is partnered with an older teacher? In some cultures, age is highly valued, and the parents may take suggestions only from the older teacher. This may create tension between co-teachers, especially if the older teacher is less experienced in a given area than the younger teacher. Note, too, that parents may prefer to interact with the teacher who is most like themselves, culturally, ethnically, by age, by gender, or by any other variable that the parents consciously or unconsciously deem appropriate.

As stressed throughout this book, the co-teachers must be able to openly communicate with each other regarding any issues that arise, and this includes concerns related to ethnicity and culture. The partners need to jointly problem solve how they will be sensitive to parental issues while maintaining their teamwork. Each team may have a different solution, but as long as both team members agree, difficult situations can be managed. These can be very tricky personal situations, but co-teachers are reminded that their ability to work effectively with parents is important to student success. Some parents may feel that one teacher likes their student better than the other teacher. In these cases, the parent may only feel comfortable with one of the team, so meetings with this parent may involve only one teacher; however, the teacher at the meeting must keep his or her partner in the communication loop. Try to focus on what will assist the student to achieve success.

## CONCLUSION

In a co-taught classroom, both teachers need to establish an effective and positive working relationship with parents. A central theme throughout this book is the importance of communication, trust, and respect between partners. These same principles should be applied by both co-teachers in their relationship with parents. Working with parents can present challenges in resolving differences and in recognizing the diversity of individual families.

When reviewing the chapter checklist, can you check the items as complete? Have you and your co-teacher established how often you will communicate with parents? Do you have a plan for parent conferences? Have you discussed how you will work together to resolve differences with parents? How will you and your co-teacher ensure that you are both sensitive in communicating with diverse families?

Working with parents can be challenging for all teachers; however, in a co-taught classroom these challenges must be confronted by the team. Both teachers need to ensure that a united team communicates with parents. So, while building teamwork, the team must also work to establish a positive relationship with parents. Co-teachers must become expert multitaskers to juggle all of these demands on their time and their relationship.

 ## REFLECTIONS

- Thoughtfully consider your current relationships with parents. Are these relationships positive?
- Consider the diversity in families you work with; what are your feelings about this diversity and your teaching?
- Do you have any concerns about working with parents?

 ## CONNECTIONS

Experienced co-teachers

- How do you think you are doing in communicating with parents?
- Are there any areas that you could strengthen or change?
- Have you had any difficulties in working with parents in the past, and how might you have resolved them better?

Beginning co-teachers

- How do you feel that your co-teaching team works with parents?
- How could you improve the way your co-teaching team works with parents?

Prospective co-teachers

- How often will you communicate with parents?
- What format (e-mail, newsletter, notes) do you both prefer?
- Have you created a plan for parent conferences?
- How will you ensure that both co-teachers are informed of parent concerns?

# References

Aroeste, J.L. (Writer) & Senensky, R. (Director). (1968). Is there in truth no beauty? (Television series episode). In G. Roddenberry (Executive Producer), *Star Trek*. New York: NBC Broadcasting.

Austin, V.L. (2001). Teacher's beliefs about co-teaching. *Remedial and Special Education, 22*, 245–255.

Bass, C.K. (1985). Running can modify classroom behavior. *Journal of Learning Disabilities, 18*, 160–161.

Bessette, H.J. (2008). Using students' drawings to elicit general and special educators' perceptions of co-teaching. *Teaching and Teacher Education, 24*, 1376–1396.

Bateman, B.D., & Linden, M.A. (2006). *Better IEPs: How to develop legally correct and educationally useful programs* (4th ed.). Verona, WI: Attainment.

Brody, C.M. (1994). Using co-teaching to promote reflective practice. *Journal of Staff Development, 15*(3), 32–36.

Brown, A., Campione, J., & Day, X. (1981). Learning to learn: On training students to learn from text. *Educational Researcher, 10*, 14–21.

Bulgren, J.A. (2006). Integrated content enhancement routines: Responding to the needs of adolescents with disabilities in rigorous inclusive secondary content classes. *Teaching Exceptional Children, 38*(6), 54–58.

Bulgren, J., Deshler, D.D., & Lenz, B.K. (2007). Engaging adolescents with LD in higher order thinking about history concepts using integrated content enhancement routines. *Journal of Learning Disabilities, 40*, 121–133.

Center for Universal Design. (2008). *About UD*. Retrieved January 28, 2011, from http://www.ncsu.edu/www/ncsu/design/sod5/cud/about_ud/about_ud.htm

Collett, A. (2008). Practical tips to help the collaborative process work more effectively in the school library media program. *Library Media Connection, 26*(4), 20.

Council for Exceptional Children. (2001). *Bright futures for exceptional learners: An agenda to achieve quality conditions for teaching and learning*. Reston, VA: Council for Exceptional Children.

Crisis Prevention Institute, Inc. (2009). *CPI's Nonviolent Crisis Intervention training program general information and empirical support*. Retrieved February 11, 2010, from http://www.crisisprevention.com/research/pdf/09-CPI-INT-013.pdf

De La Paz, S. (1999). Self-regulated strategy instruction in regular education settings: Improving outcomes for students with and without learning disabilities. *Learning Disabilities Research and Practice, 14*, 92–106.

deBettencourt, L.U., & Howard, L. (2007). *The effective special education teacher: A practical guide to success.* New York: Pearson.

Denavas-Walt, C., Proctor, B.D., & Lee, C.H. (2005). *Current population reports, P60-229, income, poverty, and health insurance coverage in the United States: 2004.* Washington, DC: U.S. Government Printing Office. Retrieved May 28, 2010, from http://www.census.gov/prod/2005pubs/p60-229.pdf

Devlin, P. (2008). Create effective teacher paraprofessional teams. *Intervention in School and Clinic, 44,* 41–44.

Dieker, L.A., & Murawski, W.W. (2003). Co-teaching at the secondary level: Unique issues, current trends, and suggestions for success. *High School Journal, 86*(4), 1–13.

Dyck, N., & Pemberton, J.B. (2002). A model for making decisions about text adaptations. *Intervention in School and Clinic, 38*(1), 28–35.

Edgemon, E.A., Jablonski, B.R., & Lloyd, J.W. (2006). Large-scale assessments: A teacher's guide to making decisions about accommodations. *Teaching Exceptional Children, 38*(3), 6–11.

Education Commission of the States. (2007). *National Comprehensive Center for Quality: Special education teacher certification and licensure.* Retrieved February 11, 2010, from http://mb2.ecs.org/reports/Reporttq.aspx?id=1542&map=0

Elliott, S., Kratochwill, T., & McKevitt, B. (2001). Experimental analysis of the effects of testing accommodations on the scores of students with and without disabilities. *Journal of School Psychology, 39,* 3–24.

Epstein, J.L., & Van Voorhis, F.L. (2001). More than minutes: Teachers' roles in designing homework. *Educational Psychologist, 36,* 181–193.

Family Educational Rights and Privacy Act (FERPA) of 1974, PL 93-380, 20 U.S.C., §§ 1232g et seq.

Fletcher, J.M., Fracis, D.J., O'Malley, K., Copeland, J., Mehta, P., Caldwell, C.J., et al. (2009). Effects of a bundled accommodations package on high-stakes testing for middle school students with reading disabilities. *Exceptional Children, 75,* 447–463.

Forness, S.R., Kavale, K.A., Blum. I.M., & Lloyd, J.W. (1997). Mega-analysis of meta-analyses: What works in special education and related services. *Teaching Exceptional Children, 29*(6), 4–9.

Friend, M., & Cook, L. (2007). *Interactions: Collaboration skills for school professionals* (5th ed.). New York: Pearson Education.

Fuchs, D., & Fuchs, L.S. (2005). Peer-assisted learning strategies: Promoting word recognition, fluency and reading comprehension in young children. *Journal of Special Education, 39,* 34–44.

Fuchs, D., Fuchs, L.S., & Burish, P. (2000). Peer-assisted learning strategies: An evidenced-based practice to promote reading achievement. *Learning Disabilities Research & Practice, 15,* 85–91.

Garrison-Wade, D., Sobel, D., & Fulmer, C. (2007). Inclusive leadership: Preparing principals for the role that awaits them. *Educational Leadership and Administration, 19,* 117–132. Retrieved May 8, 2010, from Education Research Complete database.

Gately, S.E. (2005). Two are better than one. *Principal Leadership (Middle School Edition), 5*(9), 36–41.

Gerber, P.J., & Popp, P.A. (1999). Consumer perspectives on the collaborative teaching model: Views of students with and without LD and their parents. *Remedial and Special Education, 20,* 288–296.

Gerber, P.J., & Popp, P.A. (2000). Making collaborative teaching more effective for academically able students: Recommendations for implementation and training. *Learning Disability Quarterly, 23,* 229–236.

Goetz, L., Gee, K., & Sailor, W. (1985). Using a behavior chain interruption strategy to teach communication skills to students with severe disabilities. *Journal of The Association for Persons with Severe Handicaps, 10,* 21–30.

Gorman, J.C. (2004). *Working with challenging parents of students with special needs.* Thousand Oaks, CA: Corwin Press.

Green, J.A. (2008, November/December). Collaborating with special education administrators. *Principal,* 12–15.

Grumbine, R., & Alden, P.B. (2006). Teaching science to students with learning disabilities. *The Science Teacher, 73*(3), 26–31.

Hallahan, D.P., Kauffman, J.M., & Pullen, P.C. (2009). *Exceptional learners: An introduction to special education* (11th ed.). Boston: Allyn & Bacon.

Hallahan, D.P., Lloyd, J.W., Kauffman, J.M., Weiss, M.P., & Martinez, E.A. (2005). *Learning disabilities: Foundations, characteristics, and effective teaching* (3rd ed.). New York: Pearson.

Hang, Q., & Rabren, K. (2009). An examination of co-teaching: Perspectives and efficacy indicators. *Remedial and Special Education, 30,* 259–268.

Hines, J. (2008). Making collaboration work in inclusive high school classrooms: Recommendations for principals. *Intervention in School and Clinic, 43,* 277–282. Retrieved May 8, 2010, from Education Research Complete database.

Howard, L., & James, A. (2003). *What principals need to know about . . . differentiated instruction.* Arlington, VA: Educational Research Service and National Association of Elementary School Principals.

Howard, L., &. Potts, E.A. (2009). Using co-planning time: Strategies for a successful co-teaching marriage. *Teaching Exceptional Children Plus, 5*(4), Article 2.

Hughes, C.A., Ruhl, K.L., Deshler, D.D., & Schumaker, J.B. (1993). Test-taking strategy instruction for adolescents with emotional and behavioral disorders. *Journal of Emotional and Behavioral Disorders, 1,* 189–198.

Hunkins, F., & Ornstein, A. (2009). *Curriculum: Foundations, principles, and issues* (5th ed.). Needham Heights, MA: Allyn & Bacon.

Individuals with Disabilities Education Improvement Act (IDEA) of 2004, PL 108-446, 20 U.S.C. §§ 1400 *et seq.*

Jacobs, G.M., Power, M.P., & Loh, W.I. (2002). *Teacher's sourcebook for cooperative learning: Practical techniques, basic principles, and frequently asked questions.* Thousand Oaks, CA: Corwin Press.

Jacobson, D. (2010). Coherent instructional improvement and PLCs: Is it possible to do both? *Phi Delta Kappan, 91*(6), 38–45.

Johnson, D.W., & Johnson, R.T. (1986). Mainstreaming and cooperative learning strategies. *Exceptional Children, 52,* 553–561.

Johnson, D.W., Maruyama, G., Johnson, R., Nelson, D., & Skon, L. (1981). The effects of cooperative, competitive, and individualistic goal structure on achievement: A meta-analysis. *Psychological Bulletin, 89,* 47–62.

Johnson, L.M. (2003). *What we know about: culture and learning.* Arlington, VA: Educational Research Service.

Johnson, R.T., & Johnson, D.W. (1981). Building friendships between handicapped and nonhandicapped students: Effects of cooperative and individualistic instruction. *American Educational Research Journal, 18,* 415–423. Retrieved May 17, 2010, from JSTOR database.

Joseph, N. (2010). Metacognition needed: Teaching middle and high school students to develop strategic learning skills. *Preventing School Failure, 54,* 99–103.

Kauffman, J.M. (2005). *Characteristics of emotional and behavioral disorders of children and youth* (8th ed.). New York: Pearson.

Kauffman, J.M., & Hallahan, D.P. (2005). *Special education: What it is and why we need it.* Boston: Allyn & Bacon.

Kim, A., Vaughn, S., Wanzek, J., & Wei, S. (2004). Graphic organizers and their effects on reading comprehension of students with LD: A synthesis of research. *Journal of Learning Disabilities, 37,* 105–118.

Kitmitto, S., & Bandeira de Mello, V. (2008). *Measuring the status and change of NAEP state inclusion rates for students with disabilities* (NCES 2009–453). Washington, DC: U.S. Department of Education, Institute of Education Sciences, National Center for Education Statistics.

Kloo, A., & Zigmond, N. (2008). Coteaching revisited: Redrawing the blueprint. *Preventing School Failure, 52*(2), 12–20.

Konrad, M., Helf, S., & Itoi, M. (2007). More bang for the book: Using children's literature to promote self-determination and literacy skills. *Teaching Exceptional Children, 40*(1), 64–71.

Konrad, M., Fowler, C.H., Walker, A.R., Test, D.W., & Wood, W.M. (2007). Effects of self-determination interventions on academic skills on students with learning disabilities. *Learning Disability Quarterly, 30,* 89–113.

Konrad, M., Walker, A.R., Fowler, C.H., Test, D.W., & Wood, W.M. (2008). A model for aligning self-determination and general curriculum standards. *Teaching Exceptional Children, 40*(3), 53–64.

Kosslyn, S.M., & Rosenberg, R.S. (2005). *Psychology: The brain, the person, the world.* New York: Pearson Education.

Krathwohl, D.R. (2009). *Methods of educational and social science research: The logic of methods* (3rd ed.). Long Grove, IL: Waveland Press.

Lazarus, S.S., Thurlow, M.L., Lail, K.E., & Christensen, L. (2009). A longitudinal analysis of state accommodations policies: Twelve years of change, 1993–2005. *Journal of Special Education, 43,* 67–80.

Linz, E., Heater, M.J., & Howard, L. (2008). Team teaching high school science: Game plan for success. *Teaching Exceptional Children Plus, 5*(2), Article 1.

Lloyd, J.W., Forness, S.R., & Kavale, K.A. (1998). Some methods are more effective than others. *Intervention in School and Clinic, 33,* 195–200.

Magiera, K.A., & Simmons, R.J. (2005). *Guidebook for the Magiera-Simmons quality indicator model of co-teaching.* Fredonia, NY: Excelsior Educational Services.

Magiera, K., Smith, C., Zigmond, N., & Gerbaner, K. (2005). Benefits of co-teaching in secondary mathematics classes. *Teaching Exceptional Children, 37*(3), 20–24.

Magiera, K., & Zigmond, N. (2005). Co-teaching in middle school classrooms under routine conditions: Does the instructional experience differ for students with disabilities in co-taught and solo-taught classes? *Learning Disabilities Research and Practice, 20*(2), 79–85.

Manning, M.L., & Bucher, K.T. (2003). *Classroom management: Models, applications, and cases.* Upper Saddle River, NJ: Merrill/Prentice Hall.

Marzano, R. (2003). *Classroom management that works: Research-based strategies for every teacher.* Alexandria, VA: Association for Curriculum and Development.

Marzano, R.J., & Pickering, D.J. (2007). Special topic: The case for and against homework. *Educational Leadership, 64*(6), 74–79.

Mastropieri, M.A., & Scruggs, T.E. (2001). Promoting inclusion in secondary classrooms. *Learning Disability Quarterly, 24,* 265–274.

Mastropieri, M.A, & Scruggs, T.E. (2010). *The inclusive classroom: Strategies for effective instruction* (4th ed.). New York: Pearson.

Mastropieri, M.A., Scruggs, T.E., Graetz, J., Norland, J., Gardizi, W., & McDuffie, K. (2005). Case studies in co-teaching in the content areas: Successes, failures, and challenges. *Intervention in School and Clinic, 40,* 260–270.

McDuffie, K.A. (2010). *The co-teaching guide for special education administrators: From guesswork to what really works.* Horsham, PA: LRP.

McGahee, M., Mason, C., Wallace, T., & Jones, B. (2001). *Student-led IEPs: A guide for student involvement.* Arlington, VA: Council for Exceptional Children. (ERIC Document Reproduction Service No. ED455623)

McMillan, J.H. (2003). *The relationship between instructional and classroom practices of elementary teachers and student scores on high-stakes tests.* (ERIC Document Reproduction Services No. ED472164)

Meloy, L.L., Deville, C., & Frisbie, D. (2002). The effect of read aloud accommodations on test scores of students with and without a learning disability in reading. *Remedial and Special Education, 23,* 248–255.

Mitchell, A., & Arnold, M. (2004). Behavior management skills as predictors of retention among south Texas special educators. *Journal of Instructional Psychology, 31,* 214–219.

Murawksi, W.M. (2005, Winter). Addressing diverse needs through co-teaching: Take baby steps. *Kappa Delta Pi Record,* 77–87.

Murawksi, W.M., & Dieker, L. (2008). 50 ways to keep your co-teacher: Strategies for before, during, and after co-teaching. *Teaching Exceptional Children, 40,* 40–48.

Murawski, W.W., & Hughes, C.E. (2009). Response to intervention, collaboration, and co-teaching: A logical combination for successful systemic change. *Preventing School Failure, 53,* 267–277.

Murawski, W.W., & Swanson, H.L. (2001). A meta-analysis of co-teaching research: Where are the data? *Remedial and Special Education, 22,* 258–267.

Murray, C., & Pianta, R.C. (2007). The importance of teacher-student relationships for adolescents with high incidence disabilities. *Theory into Practice, 46,* 105–112.

National Dissemination Center for Children with Disabilities. (2005). *Behavior plans.* Retrieved May 24, 2010, from http://www.nichcy.org/pages/behavassess.aspx#bip

National Joint Committee on Learning Disabilities. (2005). *PowerPoint presentation on response to intervention.* Retrieved July 18, 2009, from http://www.ncld.org

National Science Teachers Association. (1996). *National science education standards.* Retrieved July 18, 2009, from http://www.nap.edu/openbook.php?isbn=0309053269

No Child Left Behind Act of 2001, PL 107-110, 115 Stat. 1425, 20 U.S.C. §§ 6301 *et seq.*

O'Connor, M.P. (2009). Service works! Promoting transition success for students with disabilities through participation in service learning. *Teaching Exceptional Children, 41*(6), 12–17.

Orwell, G. (1993). *Animal farm.* New York: Everyman's Library. (Original work published 1946)

PACER Center. (2003). School accommodations and modifications can make a difference. *Exceptional Parent, 33*(12), 72–77.

Palmer, P.J. (1998). *The courage to teach: Exploring the inner landscape of a teacher's life.* San Francisco: Jossey-Bass.

Patterson, J., & Protheroe, N. (2000). *Essentials for principals: The school leader's guide to special education.* Alexandria, VA: Educational Research Service.

Paugh, P., Carey, J., King-Jackson, V., & Russell, S. (2007). Negotiating the literacy block: Constructing spaces for critical literacy in a high stakes setting. *Language Arts, 85*(1), 31–42.

Porter, C. (2009). Words, words, words: Reading Shakespeare with English language learners. *English Journal, 99*(1), 44–49.

Protheroe, N. (2001). *Essentials for principals: Meeting the challenges of high-stakes testing.* Arlington, VA: Educational Research Service and National Association of Elementary School Principals.

Putnam, J.W. (1998). *Cooperative learning and strategies for inclusion: Celebrating diversity in the classroom* (2nd ed.). Baltimore: Paul H. Brookes Publishing Co.

Rea, P.J., & Connel, J. (2005a). A guide to co-teaching. *Principal Leadership (High School Edition), 5*(9), 36–41.

Rea, P.J., & Connell, J. (2005b). Minding the fine points of co-teaching. *Educational Digest, 71*(1), 29–35.

Reblin, P.A. (1994). *A first-grade inclusion model that trains classroom teachers to modify and develop curriculum for language-learning disabled students.* Unpublished doctoral dissertation, Nova Southeastern University. (ERIC Document Reproduction Services No. ED374605)

Rooney, K.J., Hallahan, D.P., & Lloyd, J.W. (1984). Self-recording of attention by learning disabled students in the regular classroom. *Journal of Learning Disabilities, 17,* 360–364.

Rooney, K.J., Polloway, E.A., & Hallahan, D.P. (1985). The use of self-monitoring procedures with low IQ learning disabled students. *Journal of Learning Disabilities, 18,* 384–389.

Sabornie, E.J., & deBettencourt, L.U. (2004). *Teaching students with mild and high-incidence disabilities at the secondary level* (2nd ed.). Upper Saddle River, NJ: Merrill/Prentice Hall.

Scruggs, T.E., Mastropieri, M.A., & McDuffie, K.A. (2007). Co-teaching in inclusive classrooms: A meta-synthesis of qualitative research. *Exceptional Children, 73,* 392–416.

Smith, S.G., English, R., Vasek, D. (2002). Student and parent involvement in the transition process for college freshmen with learning disabilities. *College Student Journal, 36,* 491–503.

Sonnier-York, C., & Stanford, P. (2002). Learning to cooperate: A teacher's perspective. *Teaching Exceptional Children, 34*(6), 40–44.

Soukup, J.H., Wehmeyer, M.L., Bashinski, S.M., & Bovaird, J.A. (2007). Classroom variables and access to the general curriculum for students with disabilities. *Exceptional Children, 74,* 101–120.

Spinelli, C.G. (2006). *Classroom assessment for students in special and general education* (2nd ed.). New York: Pearson.

Steele, M.M. (2007). Helping middle school students with learning disabilities pass the federally mandated science tests: Science instruction, study skills, and test-taking strategies. *Science Scope, 31*(3), 74–80.

Tomlinson, C.A. (1999). *The differentiated classroom: Responding to the needs of all learners.* Alexandria, VA: Association for Supervision and Curriculum Development.

Ury, W. (1991). *Getting past no: Negotiating your way from confrontation to cooperation.* New York: Bantam.

U.S. Department of Education. (2005). *No Child Left Behind.* Retrieved July 20, 2009, from http://www.ed.gov/policy/elsec/guid/edpicks.jhtml?src=ln

U.S. Department of Education. (2010a). *Family Educational Rights and Privacy Act policy guidance.* Retrieved May 24, 2010, from http://www2.ed.gov/policy/gen/guid/fpco/ferpa/index.html

U.S. Department of Education. (2010b). *Race to the Top.* Retrieved October 10, 2010, from http://www.ed.gov/news/press-releases/us-education-department-awards-grants-improve-assessments-students-disabilities

U.S. Department of Education, National Center for Education Statistics. (2008). *Education and certification qualifications of departmentalized public high school-level teachers of core subjects* (NCES 2008-338). Retrieved July 20, 2009, from http://nces.ed.gov/fastfacts

Virginia Department of Education Standards of Learning. (2003). *Science standards of learning for Virginia Public Schools: Standard 5.4* (p. 17). Retrieved July 18, 2009, from http://www .doe.virginia.gov/testing/sol/standards_docs/history_socialscience/index.shtml

Virginia Department of Education Standards of Learning. (2008). *Virginia standards of learning and common core state standards.* Retrieved April 18, 2011, from http://www.doe.virginia.gov/ testing/common_core/index.shtml

Wadsworth, D.E., & Knight, D. (1996). Paraprofessionals: The bridge to successful full inclusion. *Intervention in School and Clinic, 31,* 166–171.

Walther-Thomas, C.S. (1997). Co-teaching experiences: The benefits and problems that teachers and principals report over time. *Journal of Learning Disabilities, 30,* 395–407.

Wang, M.C., Haertel, G.D., & Walberg, H.J. (1993). Toward a knowledge base for school learning. *Review of Educational Research, 63,* 249–294.

Wehmeyer, M.L., Agran, M., & Hughes, C. (1998). *Teaching self-determination to students with disabilities: Basic skills for successful transition.* Baltimore: Paul H. Brookes Publishing Co.

Wiggins, G., & McTighe, J. (2005). *Understanding by design* (2nd ed.). Alexandria, VA: Association for Supervision and Curriculum Development.

# A

# Reader's Guide

## How to Co-Teach

### *A Guide for General and Special Educators*

### HOW TO USE THIS GUIDE

This guide is designed to help you make additional connections between the content of the book and your real-life experience. Answer the questions in a large group—such as a professional learning community—with your co-teacher or by yourself. The guide consists of three parts: Thought Questions, Practice, and a K-W-L.

*Thought Questions* encourage consideration of the material as a co-teacher and link directly to the reading. We encourage you to thoughtfully reflect on each chapter and how ideas may be used in your classroom by creating additional questions related to your individual teaching practice.

*Practice* activities outline a direct and immediate way to put the content into action.

The *K-W-L* outlines your experiences with the text. First, reflect on what you already *know* about co-teaching, then what you *want* to know about co-teaching. After reading, reflect on what you have *learned* about co-teaching. This will help you self-manage professional development on co-teaching. A blank K-W-L chart is provided at the end of this appendix and on the accompanying DVD. If you are working in a large group,

1.  Identify each reader's experience with co-teaching. Ask readers

    Are you preparing to co-teach?

    Are you currently co-teaching?

2.  Begin with a K-W-L for each reader.

    What do readers *know* about co-teaching?

    What do readers *want* to know about co-teaching?

    Leave a blank space for what readers have *learned* about co-teaching (to be filled in as readers read the book).

    Provide a blank K-W-L chart that could be reproduced.

3.  Answer Thought Questions (questions designed to promote discussion).

    Each chapter has two questions.

    Readers are encouraged to create additional questions related to their individual teaching practice. They should thoughtfully reflect on the chapter and how ideas might be used in their own teaching.

## CHAPTER 1: THE BASICS OF CO-TEACHING

### Thought Questions

1.  How does the description of co-teaching in the chapter relate to your own experience of co-teaching?
2.  After considering the different models of co-teaching, please describe which model is most appealing to you and why. Which model(s) are most appropriate for which type of instruction, and how does this relate to how you teach?
3.  Thoughtfully consider the reading, then compose your own question about co-teaching and your teaching. Explore your question as you discuss the reading.

### Practice

Observe other co-teachers in your school or school division. Note the models they use, how they make those models work for their situation, and how you could incorporate practices from their classroom into your co-teaching.

### K-W-L

What did you *learn* from this chapter that is most relevant to you? Fill in the *L* in the K-W-L chart.

## CHAPTER 2: WHAT EACH TEACHER BRINGS
### Thought Questions

1. Considering the scope and sequence of the curriculum, how does the general education teacher manage to balance these demands with daily teaching?
2. Considering the varying needs of individual learners, how does the special education teacher manage both the paperwork and meeting these needs daily?
3. Thoughtfully consider the reading, then compose your own question about co-teaching and your teaching. Explore your question as you discuss the reading.

### Practice

List teaching skills and areas that you are more and less comfortable with. Use this list to begin a conversation with your co-teacher about roles in the classroom.

### K-W-L

What did you *learn* from this chapter that is most relevant to you? Fill in the *L* in the K-W-L chart.

## CHAPTER 3: BECOMING CO-TEACHERS
### Thought Questions

1. If you have chosen to co-teach, please describe why you want to co-teach and any reasons for choosing your co-teacher.
2. If you were assigned to co-teach, please describe how you will build a relationship with your co-teacher.
3. Thoughtfully consider the reading, then compose your own question about co-teaching and your teaching. Explore your question as you discuss the reading.

### K-W-L

What did you *learn* from this chapter that is most relevant to you? Fill in the *L* in the K-W-L chart.

## CHAPTER 4: GENERAL COMMUNICATION ADVICE
### Thought Questions

1. How do you deal with confrontation and uncomfortable personal situations? Spend some time becoming aware of your natural inclinations

when dealing with conflict so that you are better able to deal with potential conflict with your co-teacher.

2.  Please identify three or four items you feel are most important to your
    success as a teacher. This might be something simple, such as being able
    to locate your stapler and scissors, or something more complex, such
    as knowing how you will assess a student's writing. What might you
    be willing to compromise on? What is nonnegotiable?

3.  Thoughtfully consider the reading, then compose your own question
    about co-teaching and your teaching. Explore your question as you
    discuss the reading.

## Practice

Complete the Teaching Beliefs Questionnaire, Box 4.1 in Chapter 4. If you
are co-teaching, please discuss your responses with your teaching partner.

## K-W-L

What did you *learn* from this chapter that is most relevant to you? Fill in
the *L* in the K-W-L chart.

## CHAPTER 5: THE IDEAL VERSUS THE REALITY

### Thought Questions

1.  Describe how you and your co-teacher use your planning time.

2.  Consider how you will address conflicts or difficult issues. If you are
    already co-teaching, describe how you have resolved conflicts. If you
    are planning to co-teach, what are some specific strategies you can use
    to address points of disagreement?

3.  Thoughtfully consider the reading, then compose your own question
    about co-teaching and your teaching. Explore your question as you
    discuss the reading.

## Practice

With your co-teacher, brainstorm what you want an administrator observing your classroom to look for. What do you want him or her to know
before coming into your classroom to observe?

## K-W-L

What did you *learn* from this chapter that is most relevant to you? Fill in
the *L* in the K-W-L chart.

## CHAPTER 6: CO-TEACHERS: BEGINNING THE CONVERSATION

### Thought Questions

1.  Review the Co-Teaching Planning Checklist on page 68 and the accompanying DVD and discuss how you can incorporate this type of organizer into your planning time.
2.  What items or issues would be appropriate to discuss with your co-teacher before the start of school?
3.  Thoughtfully consider the reading, then compose your own question about co-teaching and your teaching. Explore your question as you discuss the reading.

### K-W-L

What did you *learn* from this chapter that is most relevant to you? Fill in the *L* in the K-W-L chart.

## CHAPTER 7: ASSESSMENT TO GUIDE INSTRUCTION AND GRADING

### Thought Questions

1.  Consider your philosophy of grading and discuss your perspective.
2.  Describe three different ways that a unit grade could be assessed, and describe how you can incorporate more than a single unit test for a grade.
3.  Thoughtfully consider the reading, then compose your own question about co-teaching and your teaching. Explore your question as you discuss the reading.

### Practice

Devise three ways to assess the same skill. Use the assessments in your classroom.

### K-W-L

What did you *learn* from this chapter that is most relevant to you? Fill in the *L* in the K-W-L chart.

## CHAPTER 8: ACCOMMODATIONS AND MODIFICATIONS

### Thought Questions

1.  Identify three accommodations that are commonly used in special education. Describe how you can use these accommodations in your teaching to benefit all of the learners in your class.

2.  Identify three testing accommodations that are commonly used in special education. How can you incorporate these into your classroom?

3.  Thoughtfully consider the reading, then compose your own question about co-teaching and your teaching. Explore your question as you discuss the reading.

## Practice

Use the Assessment Accommodations Decision-Making Flow Chart (see Figure 8.1) at your next IEP meeting.

## K-W-L

What did you *learn* from this chapter that is most relevant to you? Fill in the *L* in the K-W-L chart.

## CHAPTER 9: LET'S TEACH!

### Thought Questions

1.  Consider an agenda or outline for a single instructional period; which teacher will perform a specific task (e.g., collect the homework, introduce new concepts)?

2.  Describe your classroom management plan.

3.  Thoughtfully consider the reading, then compose your own question about co-teaching and your teaching. Explore your question as you discuss the reading.

## Practice

Set up your substitute teacher folder with co-teaching in mind. What does a substitute need to know about your co-taught classroom? About his or her role in the classroom when you are out? What should he or she expect when interacting with the co-teacher and students?

## K-W-L

What did you *learn* from this chapter that is most relevant to you? Fill in the *L* in the K-W-L chart.

## CHAPTER 10: INSTRUCTION IN ELEMENTARY CLASSROOMS

### Thought Questions

1.  How will you and your co-teacher ensure that a variety of instructional strategies will be used?

2. Who will be responsible for ensuring that the scope and sequence of the curriculum is addressed through different strategies?

3. Thoughtfully consider the reading, then compose your own question about co-teaching and your teaching. Explore your question as you discuss the reading.

## Practice

Incorporate one of the strategies from this chapter into your next lesson.

## K-W-L

What did you *learn* from this chapter that is most relevant to you? Fill in the *L* in the K-W-L chart.

## CHAPTER 11: INSTRUCTION IN MIDDLE AND HIGH SCHOOL

### Thought Questions

1. How will you use texts in your co-taught class? How will you provide supports to students for whom the text is not useful?

2. How will you incorporate IEP transition goals into your co-taught classroom instruction?

3. Thoughtfully consider the reading, then compose your own question about co-teaching and your teaching. Explore your question as you discuss the reading.

## Practice

Incorporate self-advocacy skills into your next lesson.

## K-W-L

What did you *learn* from this chapter that is most relevant to you? Fill in the *L* in the K-W-L chart.

## CHAPTER 12: HOW ARE WE DOING?

### Thought Questions

1. How will you and your co-teacher evaluate your relationship (e.g., discuss the relationship, gather student achievement data)?

2. How will you and your co-teacher review lesson plans to make changes or additions to be used in future teaching?

3. Thoughtfully consider the reading, then compose your own question about co-teaching and your teaching. Explore your question as you discuss the reading.

### Practice

Use student data, the Co-Teaching Self-Assessment on page 163 and the accompanying DVD, and discussion with your co-teacher to assess the efficacy of your co-teaching this year. Set goals for future co-teaching.

### K-W-L

What did you *learn* from this chapter that is most relevant to you? Fill in the *L* in the K-W-L chart.

## CHAPTER 13: WORKING WITH OTHERS IN THE SCHOOL

### Thought Questions

1. How should you and your co-teacher involve administrators in your co-teaching (e.g., invite them to visit your classroom to see a successful lesson, seek their advice when there is a problem)? How involved do you want your administrator to be? Do you need to advocate for more planning time?
2. How will you and your co-teacher ensure that there is timely communication with other professionals in your school (e.g., let the speech therapist know a field trip is coming, communicate materials needs to the IA)?
3. Thoughtfully consider the reading, then compose your own question about co-teaching and your teaching. Explore your question as you discuss the reading.

### K-W-L

What did you *learn* from this chapter that is most relevant to you? Fill in the *L* in the K-W-L chart.

## CHAPTER 14: WORKING WITH PARENTS

### Thought Questions

1. How will you and your co-teacher communicate to parents that you are both responsible for instruction, grading, and classroom management? (Consider such communication opportunities as Back-to-School Night and parent newsletters—how do you present yourselves as co-equal teaching partners?)
2. How will you and your co-teacher respond to unhappy or angry parents?
3. Thoughtfully consider the reading, then compose your own question about co-teaching and your teaching. Explore your question as you discuss the reading.

## Practice

Create a shared Parent Contact Log, such as the one provided in Chapter 14 (see Figure 14.2), and discuss with your co-teacher how you will jointly use it.

## K-W-L

What did you *learn* from this chapter that is most relevant to you? Fill in the *L* in the K-W-L chart.

## PLAN FOR CO-TEACHING

Once you have finished the book, consider creating a personal co-teaching plan. You might want to use a school-year calendar and note times to discuss students, discuss co-teaching, work on new strategies, and evaluate your co-teaching relationship. Co-teaching can be an exciting adventure, but it helps to have a plan to successfully navigate through the school year!

# K-W-L Chart

| K<br>What do you *KNOW* about co-teaching? | W<br>What do you *WANT* to know<br>about co-teaching? | L<br>What have you *LEARNED*<br>about co-teaching? |
| --- | --- | --- |
| | | |

*How to Co-Teach: A Guide for General and Special Educators* by Elizabeth A. Potts & Lori A. Howard

# B

# DVD Guide

## HOW TO USE THIS GUIDE

With your co-teacher

- Watch the DVD together.
- Discuss the "What should I watch for on the DVD?" questions.
- Reflect together on how your co-teaching relationship is like or unlike the situation presented. How can you use the situation presented to improve your combined practice?

For individual professional development

- Watch the DVD.
- Reflect on the "What should I watch for on the DVD?" questions.
- Where appropriate, create action items for yourself, such as "Talk with my co-teacher about gum and food policies."

For group professional development

- Watch the DVD together.
- Discuss the "What should I watch for on the DVD?" questions.
- Discuss the process depicted in the clips. What is good practice? What could be done to improve on the things that are not good practice? How can your professional development team support strong co-teaching?

## CHAPTER 1

 ### *WHAT'S ON THE DVD?*

This is a sample co-taught lesson that follows the Team Teaching format.

 ### *WHAT SHOULD I WATCH FOR ON THE DVD?*

- Can you determine which teacher is the content expert? Why or why not?
- What do these teachers do that helps them present themselves to the class as a team?

## CHAPTER 2

 ### *WHAT'S ON THE DVD?*

Sherry, a general educator, talks about how her co-teacher, Craig, helps her teach more effectively—offering rewording for immediate clarification, different ways of thinking, and additional approaches that make concepts more accessible by presenting several angles.

 ### *WHAT SHOULD I WATCH FOR ON THE DVD?*

- How do these co-teachers' strengths play together to benefit their students?
- What kinds of ideas and input do you think a co-teacher can bring to your classroom to improve instruction?

## CHAPTER 3

 ### *WHAT'S ON THE DVD?*

Sherry and Craig talk about how they began co-teaching, their shared philosophy, and planning practices.

 ### *WHAT SHOULD I WATCH FOR ON THE DVD?*

- What do these co-teachers do that makes them successful?
- How can I talk with my co-teacher about working toward a shared philosophy for our classroom?

## CHAPTER 4

 *WHAT'S ON THE DVD?*

Sherry talks about how, as a general education teacher, she struggled with sharing control but learned to become comfortable in trusting her special education co-teacher, Craig. Sherry and Craig talk about the benefits of having a male and a female co-teacher in the classroom.

Tom, a special educator whose identity is protected in the DVD because he has not had good co-teaching experiences, talks about how he and his co-teacher found a way to teach together, regardless of their feelings about working together.

Ed and Tom talk about having difficult conversations with a co-teacher.

 *WHAT SHOULD I WATCH FOR ON THE DVD?*

- How did Sherry and Craig's co-teaching change as they gained trust in each other?
- How does having a common goal or philosophy with your co-teacher affect your classroom?
- What would be the best way for you to approach your co-teacher with a potential conflict? How can you present yourself in order to not appear confrontational?
- What is (or will be) hard for you to do, related to communicating with your co-teacher?

## CHAPTER 5

 *WHAT'S ON THE DVD?*

Sherry talks about the support she and her co-teacher have received from administration to help them continue to teach together for several years.

Debbie, an administrator, talks about what good co-teaching looks like in the classroom and how co-teachers can improve their relationship.

Craig talks about the reality of co-teaching with multiple general education teachers.

 *WHAT SHOULD I WATCH FOR ON THE DVD?*

- How can administrators help co-teachers work through the realities of co-teaching?
- How does Craig organize working with more than one co-teacher?

*Note:* There are no DVD video clips for Chapter 6.

## CHAPTER 7

 ### *WHAT'S ON THE DVD?*

Ed and MJ talk about how they make grading transparent between themselves and the students.

 ### *WHAT SHOULD I WATCH FOR ON THE DVD?*

- How does Ed and MJ's practice help students succeed? How does Ed and MJ's practice reflect their philosophy that the class is *their* shared class?

## CHAPTER 8

 ### *WHAT'S ON THE DVD?*

Sherry and Craig talk about how they adjust instruction to meet the needs of students by limiting the curriculum and providing accommodations in the large group.

 ### *WHAT SHOULD I WATCH FOR ON THE DVD?*

- What accommodations does this co-teaching team provide?

## CHAPTER 9

 ### *WHAT'S ON THE DVD?*

MJ and Ed give advice related to what co-teachers need to talk about before the school year begins.

 ### *WHAT SHOULD I WATCH FOR ON THE DVD?*

- Have you and your co-teacher talked about the things that Ed and MJ list?
- How would you have handled the situation that Ed describes with his previous co-teacher and the student who was chewing gum?
- Do you have a syllabus for your class? Does it reflect the ideas Ed talked about?

## CHAPTER 10

 *WHAT'S ON THE DVD?*

Ed and MJ describe, for their active physics class, the mnemonic *PIES*.

 *WHAT SHOULD I WATCH FOR ON THE DVD?*

- What co-teaching model are Ed and MJ using in this clip?
- What makes this an effective instructional technique?

## CHAPTER 11

 *WHAT'S ON THE DVD?*

Sherry and Craig talk about how they share instructional and planning responsibilities.

 *WHAT SHOULD I WATCH FOR ON THE DVD?*

- How do Sherry and Craig's decisions about the split in workload reflect each co-teacher's strengths? How do the decisions reflect each co-teacher's likes and dislikes?
- Do you consider strengths, likes, and dislikes when you and your co-teacher plan?

## CHAPTER 12

 *WHAT'S ON THE DVD?*

Ed talks about formative assessment and making improvements in instruction from one year to the next.

Sherry and Craig talk about their reflection process and how they measure their success.

 *WHAT SHOULD I WATCH FOR ON THE DVD?*

- What changes from one year to the next does Ed talk about?
- How do Sherry and Craig determine if their co-teaching is successful?

## CHAPTER 13

 *WHAT'S ON THE DVD?*

Debbie, an administrator, talks about a master schedule that supports co-teaching and offers advice to administrators of schools with co-teaching.

Debbie talks about how she, as an administrator, mediates co-teachers who are not getting along.

Tom, a special educator whose identity is protected in the DVD because he has not had good co-teaching experiences, talks about how he and his co-teacher with whom he does not have a good working relationship make it work.

 *WHAT SHOULD I WATCH FOR ON THE DVD?*

- Does your administrator share the same philosophy as Debbie?
- What tactics does Tom use to make his co-teaching situation as successful as possible?

## CHAPTER 14

 *WHAT'S ON THE DVD?*

Craig and Sherry talk about how they communicate with parents.

 *WHAT SHOULD I WATCH FOR ON THE DVD?*

- This method made the most sense for this co-teaching pair. What makes sense for you?

# Index

Page numbers followed by *b* indicate boxes. Those followed by *f* indicate figures or forms, and those followed by *t* indicate tables.